CHILD'S BIBLE

Text by Rosa Mediani
Illustrations by Silvia Colombo

Paulist Press
New York / Mahwah, NJ

Cover design by Laura Sansotera
Book design by Giuseppe Oggioni

Originally published as *La Bibbia Raccontata al Ragazzi* by Edizioni San Paolo s.r.l.
Copyright © 2018 by EDIZIONI SAN PAOLO s.r.l.
Piazza Soncino, 5 – 20092 Cinisello Balsamo (Milan)
www.edizionisanpaolo.it

English translation by Demetrio S. Yocum
Copyright © 2019 by Paulist Press, Inc.

Library of Congress Control Number: 2018962607

ISBN 978-0-8091-6791-3 (paperback)

Published in the United States of America by
Paulist Press
997 Macarthur Boulevard
Mahwah, NJ 07430
www.paulistpress.com

Printed and bound in Slovenia
By GRAFOSTIL D.O.O.
December 2018

BEFORE YOU START READING

Dear Children,

This edition of the Bible, prepared especially for you, expresses the mission of Edizioni San Paolo: to live and communicate to everyone, in the most diverse ways, the Word that God has addressed to the world.

What you have in your hands is not another "illustrated Bible." There are plenty of those on the market. This Bible has some special features:

- First of all, we wanted to tell not only the most well-known stories of the Bible—such as the Creation of the World, the Great Flood, the Crossing of the Red Sea—but also those that are perhaps less known to you but that are part of the thread of God's love for his people, even when the Lord had to face the frailties, unkindness, and disobedience of Israel.
- Second, we wanted the illustrations to be a kind of "first description" of the text, where even the details help you to reflect, to think, and to understand.
- Finally, we have tried to show how the individual books of the Bible form a single story within which we—including you—have a role to play.

Our founder, Blessed James Alberione, loved to say that the Bible is a beautiful letter that God has written to humanity and that it would be a shame to let the years go by without reading it, or worse, without even opening it. I hope this edition can help you to grasp its beauty and power because, today and tomorrow, the Bible can be your traveling companion, along with God who dwells in every line.

Enjoy your reading.

Fr. Valdir José De Castro
Superior General, Society of Saint Paul

Valdir José De Castro

OLD
TESTAMENT

SIX DAYS OF CREATION

In the beginning, the earth was an empty space and without shape. Darkness and water covered it and the Spirit of God hovered above all. On the first day God said, "Let there be light." And the light broke into the frightening darkness, driving it away.

The Lord then separated the light from the darkness. He called the light "day" and the darkness "night."

On the second day, God created the heavenly dome. Clouds appeared for the first time in the sky, and rain and snow fell from the clouds.

On the third day, God gathered the water and called it "the sea," and brought out the dry land, which he called "Earth." Thus the oceans and the continents were born. The ground was covered with grasses, flowers, and fruit plants. The trees rose to the sky and the forests covered the earth.

On the fourth day, God created immense lights in the sky: the sun to give light to the day, and the moon and the stars to illuminate the night.

On the fifth day, God created the animals that live in the water and those that live in the air. Fish of all kinds swam in the seas, rivers, and lakes, and flocks of birds flew through the air.

On the sixth day, God said, "Let the earth be inhabited by living beings of every species." And the wild and domestic animals appeared, from the very small to the very large.

The earth was now ready to welcome human beings. God said, "Let us make humans in our image and likeness." Thus God created man and woman and blessed them and said, "Love one another and be fruitful. Inhabit the earth and give a name to every creature."

The first man was called Adam and the first woman Eve.

God saw that everything he had created was good.

His work was finished.

On the seventh day, God did not work and dedicated it to rest.

ADAM AND EVE IN THE GARDEN OF EDEN

God planted a garden in the east. He put Adam and Eve there to live, to cultivate it and keep it. The garden was surrounded by four rivers, and from the ground sprouted plants that produced good fruit to eat. In the middle of the garden there were two trees: the tree of life and the tree of knowledge of good and evil. The man and the woman were free to eat all the fruits of the garden except those of this last tree. "Do not eat from them. Do not even touch them! Otherwise you will die." This was God's command. But the serpent, the most cunning and envious of all creatures, said to the woman, "You will not die at all! You will know what is good and evil, and you will become like God."

Eve did not resist. She took a fruit from the tree and ate it, then gave it to Adam, and he tasted it too.

When they heard the steps of the Lord in the garden, the man and the woman were afraid and ran to hide. God was waiting for them to admit their mistake, but instead they began to blame each other and accuse the serpent.

God punished them by sending them out of the garden and telling Adam, "You will earn your food by working hard" and Eve, "You will become a mother at the cost of many sufferings." And finally God told the serpent, "You will crawl on the ground, and one day you will be crushed by the son of a woman."

CAIN AND ABEL

Adam and Eve had two sons, Cain and Abel. The first worked the fields and the second grazed the flock. Both of them presented to the Lord the fruits of their work: Abel the firstlings of his flock, and Cain the common fruits of the earth. While God was pleased with Abel's offerings, he was not pleased with Cain's.

God saw jealousy grow in Cain's heart and said to him, "Why are you sad? If you do good, you will be well; but if you do wrong, your sin will not leave you alone."

But Cain's jealousy of his brother turned into hatred, until one day Cain invited Abel to follow him to the field and killed him. Scared by what he had done, Cain fled in despair. Believing himself to be in danger of death from heaven and from earth, he wandered without peace and wherever he went, he felt the invisible gaze of God upon him. But the Lord forbade anyone to kill Cain and placed a mark on him so that no one who saw him would kill him.

Cain, to defend himself, built the first city. And in the city violence became the law of its inhabitants.

THE GREAT FLOOD

When the wickedness of people reached its peak, God grieved and said, "I want to wipe out from the earth the human beings I have created."

But among many evil people there was a righteous man, Noah, whom God cared for in a special way.

God gave Noah orders to build an ark, a large ship sealed with bitumen, and to bring into the ark two of every kind of animal.

Finally, Noah's family entered the ark: his wife, his sons Shem, Ham, and Japheth, and their wives.

When everyone had entered, God himself sealed the door of the ark. Then the sky opened, and the waters of the flood came on the earth. It rained for forty days and forty nights. The rivers overflowed, the seas flooded the continents, and the waters grew so high as to cover the highest mountains. Every creature that lived on the surface of the earth died and nobody was saved. Only the ark floated on the stormy waters. Then the rain stopped, the waters began to lower, and the ark, intact, settled on the top of a mountain.

Noah sent several birds to see if the waters had subsided, one after another, until finally a dove returned to the ark with an olive branch in its beak, a sign that the waters were dried up from the earth. Then Noah came out of the ark with his family and, building an altar of stone, offered a sacrifice to thank God. The Lord liked that offering and said, "For as long as the earth will last, I will never again send such a flood." The rainbow appeared in the sky as a sign of God's promise.

THE TOWER OF BABEL

The land became lush again, and the human beings multiplied and settled in a great plain. They were one great people and they all spoke the same language.

They founded a city called Babel, built with clay bricks. At the center of the city they wanted to raise a tower so high it touched the sky. "It will be the sign of our unity and our strength," they said.

But this was not God's plan. Seeing the danger of so much pride, he decided to confuse the languages of the builders. Suddenly no one understood what the other workmate said, no one could give orders, and no one could carry them out.

The tower project was abandoned, and the people were scattered over the face of all the earth.

ABRAHAM LOOKS AT THE SKY

Among the families scattered over the face of the earth, there was the one of the descendants of Shem, son of Noah, who had settled in Haran, in Mesopotamia. His name was Abraham. God called Abraham and said to him, "Go from your country, leave your father's house and go to the land that I will show you." Abraham, who at the time of the call was already seventy-five, gathered his flocks and herdsmen and left with his wife Sarah.

When he arrived in the land of Canaan, God spoke again to Abraham, saying, "Raise your eyes and look far away. All the land you see I will give to you and your descendants." Abraham replied sadly, "Lord, what will you give me? My wife Sarah and I are old, and we have no children."

God replied, "You will have a son with Sarah. Look at the sky and count the stars if you can. As they are countless, so shall be the people born of you."

And Abraham believed in the Lord's promise.

But time passed without anything happening. Then Sarah suggested to Abraham to have a son from his slave Hagar who they would then adopt and raise. But when she was pregnant, Hagar began to feel superior to her mistress and the two women ended up quarreling. Hagar fled into the desert, but an angel of the Lord helped her near a spring and invited her to return to her mistress. Hagar gave birth to a child who was called Ishmael. But God had established that the son of the promise should be born of Sarah.

THE THREE VISITORS

On a hot day, while Abraham sat at the entrance of his tent planted at Mamre, three men suddenly appeared. Abraham went to meet them and offered his hospitality, inviting them to take some food and rest. "Sarah will have a child in a year" was the announcement of the three mysterious figures. Sarah, who was listening at the tent entrance, laughed to herself, thinking that at her age it was impossible to have a child, but they heard her and said to her, "Nothing is impossible for God."

After a year Sarah gave birth to a child. His parents called him Isaac, which means "laughter" in the language of the Bible.

After Isaac's birth, the rivalry between Sarah and Hagar began again.
Sarah insisted that her husband drive away the servant and her son.
Abraham was grieved, but he knew the Lord would take care of them.
He gave water and supplies to Hagar and sent her away with her child.
When she got lost in the desert, an angel came to her aid saying, "Do
not be afraid. I have listened to your son's tears. He will not die, and
the Lord will give him many descendants."
And he guided her to water and salvation.
    Ishmael grew and became the father of a
        large population that lived in the desert.

THE SACRIFICE OF ISAAC

When Isaac was grown, God wanted to test Abraham's faithfulness. He said to him, "Abraham! Take your son Isaac and go to the region of Moriah. On the mountain that I will show you, you will kill your child and offer him as a sacrifice." Abraham was upset by God's request, but he awakened his son and his servants; he saddled the donkey and loaded it with wood. Then he took the knife and set off. "Father," Isaac told him, "we have fire and wood, but I do not see the lamb you will offer as a sacrifice."

"God will provide," Abraham answered.

After three days of walking, they came to the mountain. Abraham built an altar with stones and laid wood there. Then he tied up Isaac, placed him on the wood, and took the knife. When he was about to strike the blow, an angel of the Lord stopped him saying, "Abraham, do not touch Isaac, do not hurt him! Now I know that you love the Lord more than anyone else."

Abraham looked up and saw a ram close by, with its horns entangled in a bush. He took the ram and offered it as a sacrifice instead of Isaac.

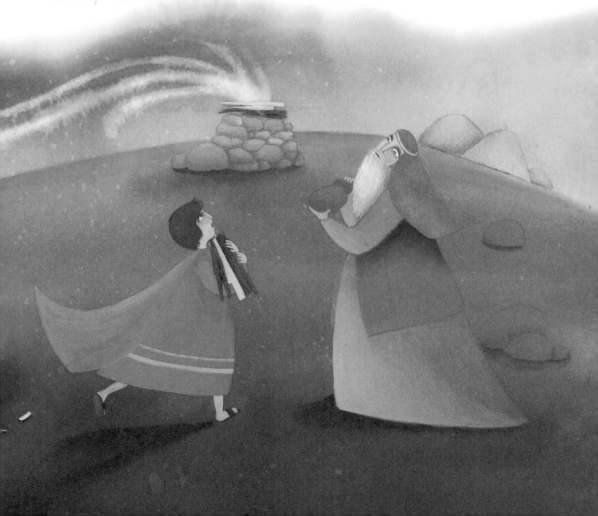

JACOB AND ESAU

When he became an adult, Isaac married a woman named Rebecca.
At the death of Abraham, he inherited his father's property. He
was a rich and happy man, but in his marriage the children were
late in coming. After long years, God answered the married couple's
prayers and twins were born: Esau and Jacob. The two brothers were
very different. Esau, the eldest, loved hunting and life in the open
air, and for this reason his father was proud of him. Jacob instead
preferred to remain in the camp and was favored by his mother.
One day Esau, returning from his hunting, found Jacob preparing a
lentil soup and said, "Give me your soup! I'm dead tired."
"First grant me your rights as the firstborn," replied Jacob.
According to tradition, the firstborn son was the heir of his father's
goods and also had God's special blessing. Esau was hungry, so he
said yes to his brother and then forgot what he said in that moment
of thoughtlessness.
Isaac, who was now old and blind, thought it was time to give his
blessing to Esau and said to his son, "Go hunting for me and prepare
some wild game. Bring it to me and I will give you my blessing."
Now Rebecca, Isaac's wife, heard everything and decided to favor
Jacob, so she sent him to get two choice goats. He quickly killed
them and cooked a tasty plate of meat. Rebecca told him, "Bring it
to your father and he will bless you." Jacob entered trembling
into Isaac's tent. His father asked him to come closer; he wanted to
touch him to make sure that it was Esau, who was very hairy.
Rebecca had foreseen this and had covered Jacob's arms
and neck with the skin of the goats. Isaac liked the food

prepared for him and said, "Give me a kiss, my son." Jacob kissed him and obtained his blessing.

Soon after, Esau returned from his hunting. He rushed to his father and, when he learned what had happened, he understood what he had given up. He burst into sobs and cried, "Father, bless me too!" But now there was nothing left to do; Isaac could not withdraw the blessing given to Jacob. Esau was furious and wanted to take revenge on his brother for his deception. Rebecca, fearing for Jacob's life, told him to flee far away:

"Go to Haran where my brother Laban lives. Find a wife there and come back only after Esau's wrath has subsided."

Jacob left and after the sun had set he stopped to sleep. He dreamed of a long ladder that reached from the earth to heaven; angels ascended and descended from the ladder, and in the dream God told him, "I am the God of Abraham and Isaac. I will give you and your children the land where you are lying, and I will protect you wherever you go." Jacob consecrated the place to the Lord and vowed loyalty to God.

THE FIGHT IN THE DARK

Having arrived at Laban's camp, Jacob fell in love with his beautiful cousin Rachel, and when he asked his uncle to marry her, Laban agreed, but in return Jacob would have to work seven years for him as a herdsman. Finally, the wedding was celebrated; but to Jacob's surprise, the bride was not Rachel but her older sister Leah. "The younger sister cannot marry before the older one," Laban said. "You have to serve me another seven years and then you can marry my other daughter too." Jacob loved Rachel very much and so he served his uncle for another seven years. He had numerous sons with Leah and only one son with Rachel, named Joseph. Jacob remained for twenty years in the service of his uncle and in all this time the Lord protected him, making him very rich.

Then the Lord said to Jacob, "Go back to your country. I will be with you." Jacob then departed with his wives, his sons, the camels, and the cattle to the land of Canaan. Jacob now had to face the wrath of his brother Esau but, on the strength of God's promise, he sent gifts to his brother to reconcile with him.

When they reached a shallow place in the river, Jacob had his family,
servants, and cattle cross to the other side. It was dark, and
when he was about to cross, a man stood before him. They wrestled
all night, and when the dawn came, the stranger asked him,
"What is your name?" "Jacob!" he said. "From now on," the man said,
"you shall be called Israel, and so will your descendants, because
you have struggled with God and you have won." Then he blessed
him. When the two brothers met, they embraced and made peace.
Jacob went to the house where his father was waiting for him.
During the journey, Rachel's second son, Benjamin, was born, but
it brought great sorrow to Jacob, because Rachel died in childbirth.

JOSEPH AND HIS BROTHERS

Among the many sons of Jacob, Joseph was the one preferred
by his father and the other brothers were jealous.
Joseph often had strange dreams. "I dreamed we were in the field
tying sheaves of wheat. Suddenly my sheaf stood up straight and
your sheaves bowed down to mine," he once said to his brothers.
Another time, Joseph said he had dreamed that the sun, the moon,
and eleven stars bowed down to him. Jacob rebuked him: "What are
these dreams? Do you think you can become a king and we all have
to bow to the ground before you?" But Jacob thought more about
it. Dreams could be prophecies sent by God. His brothers, however,
came to hate him and swore to get rid of him as soon as possible.
One day, while they were grazing the flock away from the camp,
they saw Joseph approaching. "Here comes the dreamer!" they said.
"Let us kill him and so we will see what his dreams are good for!"
But one of them said, "No! We do not want to become
guilty of a crime. Let us just throw him in a pit."
And so they did: they grabbed him, stripped him,
and threw him into an empty pit. When a caravan
of merchants headed for Egypt passed by, one
of the brothers suggested
they sell Joseph
as a slave.

They took the beautiful coat that Joseph had, dipped it in the blood of a goat, and took it to their father. Jacob, recognizing his son's long coat, burst into tears. "A wild animal has devoured my beloved son, and nothing can comfort me!" he said. From then on, Jacob poured all his affection upon Benjamin, the last born of his beloved Rachel.

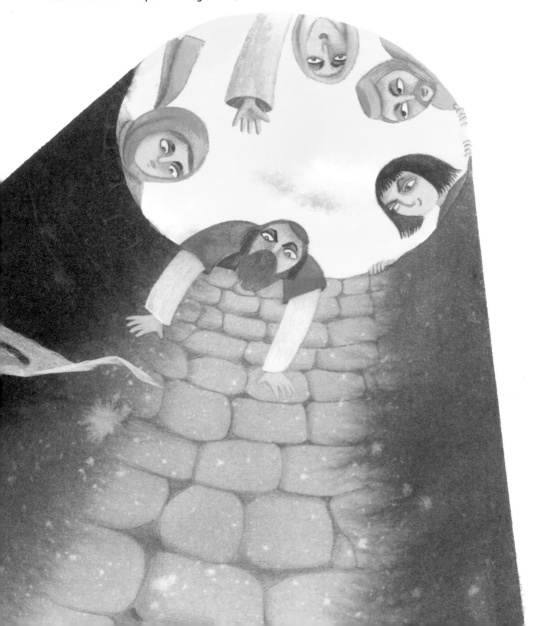

PHARAOH'S DREAMS

In Egypt, the merchants sold Joseph to Potiphar, the captain of Pharaoh's guards. Potiphar realized that the young Jewish slave was intelligent and educated, and he put Joseph in charge of taking care of everything he owned. While Joseph worked in Potiphar's home, Potiphar's wife fell in love with him. Loyal to his master, Joseph refused her proposals. But the woman, offended, accused the young man in front of her husband: "We were alone in the house and he tried to take advantage of me!" Unable to prove his innocence, Joseph was put in jail.

Pharaoh's chief cupbearer and his chief baker were also in prison. One night, they had a dream. The chief cupbearer had dreamed of pressing the grapes of a vine with three branches into Pharaoh's cup. The chief baker, on the other hand, had dreamed of carrying on his head three baskets full of bread, which was eaten by the birds. Joseph interpreted their dreams: after three days, the chief cupbearer would return to court, while the chief baker would be hanged. And so it happened.

Two years passed, and Pharaoh had a strange dream. He called his magicians, and said, "I saw seven fat cows come out of the Nile, and after them seven ugly and thin cows came out, and they devoured the fat ones. Then I saw seven ears of grain, plump and good, sprout, but then seven thin and blighted ears appeared and swallowed the seven plump and full ears."

28

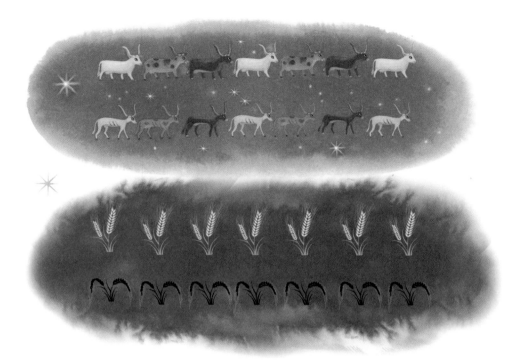

But nobody could explain the dream. Then the chief cupbearer remembered Joseph and spoke to Pharaoh. Joseph was called to court. He listened to Pharaoh's story and then said, "God is showing you what is about to happen. There will be seven years of great abundance and then seven years of terrible famine. You must choose a wise man to set aside some of the harvest in the years of plenty so there will be food to eat during the famine." Pharaoh, full of admiration for Joseph, entrusted the task to him and appointed him governor of Egypt. Joseph was thirty years old. He visited the territories of Pharaoh and built huge barns in all the cities and, during the years of abundance, he had the grain gathered there. As predicted, the years of famine followed the seven years of abundance. Then Joseph opened the granaries and saved Egypt from hunger.

THE CHILDREN OF ISRAEL IN EGYPT

The famine also struck the land of Canaan and Joseph's brothers were forced to go to Egypt to buy grain. When they arrived in the presence of the governor, they bowed before him without recognizing him. But Joseph recognized them and, to put them to the test, he treated them as spies. He questioned them and allowed them to buy grain and return home only if one of the brothers, Simeon, stayed behind as a hostage. He told them, "Come back with the youngest brother of yours, the one who stayed at home. That way I will have proof that you are not spies, and I will give you back your brother."

When Jacob learned what had happened, he despaired. "Joseph is gone, Simeon is gone," he said to his sons. "Now you want to take away Benjamin too! No, this son will not leave!" But the famine continued, and Jacob was forced to let his children return to Egypt to buy more grain and allow Benjamin to accompany them.

Joseph was waiting for them and as soon as the brothers arrived in his palace, he immediately wanted to meet Benjamin.

Then he invited them to a banquet and served them special food as a sign of goodwill. But the next day he put them on trial again, accusing them of a theft they had not committed and threatening to take Benjamin as a slave.

The brothers were shocked and feared that God's justice had struck them; they had never forgotten that they sold Joseph to the merchants as a slave. This time they refused to abandon the youngest and, when Judah offered himself a slave instead of Benjamin, Joseph realized that his brothers had really changed.

Then, moved to tears, he made himself known to his brothers: "I am Joseph! Tell me, does my father still live?" He hugged them, forgave the evil they had done to him, and invited them to settle in Egypt because the famine would last five more years.

Jacob thought he was dreaming when he was told that his favorite son was alive and was the most powerful official in Egypt. In a few days preparations for departure were made, and Jacob was able to embrace Joseph again.

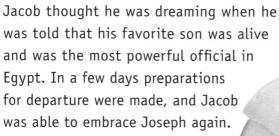

MOSES SAVED FROM THE WATERS

In Egypt, the descendants of Jacob's sons became a numerous people. A new Pharaoh, who had forgotten how much Joseph had done to save the kingdom from famine and fearing that the Israelites could become more powerful than the Egyptians, made them slaves and forced them to work in the construction of his cities. But despite the hard work, the people of Israel continued to grow.

So Pharaoh ordered that every newborn Israelite male was to be thrown into the Nile River. One mother, however, managed to hide her baby, and to save it she laid it in a basket sealed with bitumen and deposited it among the rushes of the Nile.

When Pharaoh's daughter came down to the Nile with her maidservants, she saw the basket and the crying baby. She thought, "He is a one of the Israelites' children," and she had compassion for him. She called him Moses, which means "saved from out of the waters," and she raised him as her son.

When he became an adult, Moses went to visit the construction sites where the Israelites worked as slaves. But when he saw an Egyptian beat a Hebrew, he struck the Egyptian so hard that he killed him. Frightened by the consequences of his action, Moses fled far away where the punishment of the Pharaoh could not reach him.

Arriving in the land of Midian, he put himself at the service of the priest Jethro and married one of his daughters, Zipporah.

A BURNING BUSH

One day, Moses was grazing his father-in-law's flock on Mount Horeb, when he saw a bush that was on fire, but that burned without being consumed. Amazed, he approached for a closer look and heard a voice saying, "I am the God of your fathers. I saw the sufferings of my people and I have come down to free them. Go to Pharaoh and command him to allow the Israelites to leave Egypt."
"Who am I to order Pharaoh to do such a thing?" Moses asked in alarm.
"Do not be afraid, I will be with you. I will strike Egypt with my power, and Pharaoh will have to let you leave," said the Lord.
"But what will I tell the Israelites when they ask me who sent me?"
"You will answer that I AM has sent you to bring them back to the land he had promised their fathers."
Moses obeyed, returned to Egypt, and the Lord sent his brother Aaron to accompany him in his mission. Moses explained to the Israelites that the Lord had heard their prayer and was about to free them from slavery.

THE PLAGUES

Moses and Aaron presented themselves before Pharaoh and asked him to let the Israelites leave. "Who is the Lord that I should obey his voice? And who will work in the place of these slaves of mine?" replied Pharaoh, who then ordered that the Hebrews be treated even more harshly. As God had promised, to break the pride of Pharaoh, God sent upon Egypt terrible signs of his power.

At the touch of Aaron's rod, the waters of the Nile turned into blood, the fish died, and a sickly odor rose from the river. But Pharaoh did not change his mind, and God sent another punishment: a multitude of frogs invaded the country, even sneaking into the people's houses.

Pharaoh seemed to yield, but then went back to persecuting the Israelites. Then Aaron touched the dust of the earth with his stick, and the dust became a cloud of mosquitoes. Pharaoh promised to let the Israelites leave. But once again he did not keep his promise, and immediately swarms of flies filled Egypt. The chastisements continued and were more and more painful. The Egyptians' animals became ill and horses, donkeys, camels, oxen, and sheep died in the thousands. But Pharaoh did not give up.

Moses then threw a handful of soot into the air, and instantly the skin of the Egyptians was covered with boils.

Not even the hail that fell, the swarms of locusts that devoured the crops, or the darkness that covered all of Egypt overcame Pharaoh's obstinacy. To every one of the Israelites' requests to leave Egypt, Pharaoh said no, and his heart hardened more with every new punishment.

THE PASSOVER

God said to Moses, "I will send one last punishment against Egypt, and after this, Pharaoh will let you go without conditions." He ordered every Israelite family to sacrifice and roast a lamb and to mark the doors of their houses with its blood. "You will eat it quickly, ready to leave. In the night I will pass and will strike every firstborn of the land of Egypt. Where I see the blood on the doors, I will pass over." The people of Israel did as the Lord had ordered them and they waited, wearing their traveling clothes.
At midnight, from the houses of the Egyptians, awful cries rose: the angel of the Lord had struck to death all the firstborn, from the son of Pharaoh to that of the humblest inhabitant of Egypt.
Pharaoh sent for Moses and begged him to leave with his people that same night. "Go away! Otherwise we will all die!" The Egyptians urged them to go quickly and gave them many gifts to get them to hurry.
The Israelites quickly gathered all their belongings and left Egypt, where they had lived for more than four hundred years. God had freed them from slavery and led them to a new land. That night was remembered forever as the Passover of the Lord. During the journey, an immense cloud showed them the way by day and provided light at night.

But Pharaoh regretted letting them go, and so headed out with his army in pursuit. While the people of Israel were encamped on the shores of the Red Sea, they saw the chariots of Pharaoh and his knights appear on the horizon. Moses reassured them, saying, "The Lord will fight for you today." He stretched out his hand over the sea, a strong wind rose, and the waters parted.

With two walls of water looming high on either side of them, the Israelites walked on the dry ground and reached the opposite bank.

The pursuers tried to follow them on the same path, but as soon as they were in the middle of the sea, Moses stretched out his hand again and the waters crashed in over the Egyptian army.

The people of Israel saw the power of the Lord and believed in him and in Moses.

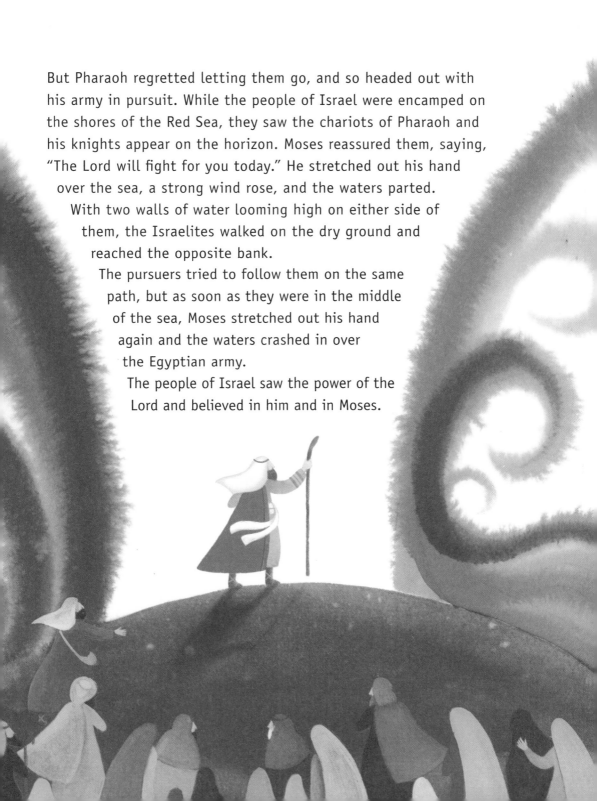

IN THE DESERT

The joy of freedom did not last long. The journey in the desert was tiring and the supplies grew scant. The Israelites began to complain to Moses and to Aaron, "When we were in Egypt we ate our fill of bread. Why have you brought us to this desert to die of hunger?" But God came to their aid. "I will send bread from heaven," he said to Moses. "In the morning everyone will have to collect as much as they need for a day." The next morning, after the dew had evaporated, on the surface of the desert there remained some white granules that tasted like flour mixed with honey. This was manna, and with it the Lord nourished the Israelites for

the whole journey toward the promised land.

But when they were thirsty, they began to protest again: "Did you lead us out of Egypt to make us die of thirst?" And God, who is patient, came to their rescue again. He ordered Moses to hit a huge rock with his staff, and when he did, so much water gushed out that it quenched the thirst of all of them.

"Is the Lord among us or not?" Moses said to them.

God did not abandon them even when they had to face Amalek and his bandits, helping them win the battle with the young Joshua as their leader. But the discomforts of the journey upset the Israelites, who continued to miss their lives as slaves back in Egypt. They did not understand that God loved them, freed them, and took care of them.

THE TEN COMMANDMENTS

Three months after leaving Egypt, they arrived in the Sinai desert at the foot of Mount Horeb, where Moses had seen the bush burning without being consumed, and here they camped.

Moses walked alone toward the top of the mountain, which was wrapped in clouds. The Lord came down to the mountain and spoke to Moses in a voice of thunder and gave him these ten commandments: "I am the Lord your God. You will have no other gods before me. You will not make idols and you will not bow down to them.

You will not use the name of the Lord wrongly.

Six days you will work, but the seventh day is consecrated to the Lord.

Honor your father and your mother.

Do not kill.

Do not commit adultery.

Do not steal.

Do not speak falsely against your neighbor.

Do not desire the house of another, neither his wife, nor his things."

Moses stayed forty days on the mountain talking with God and received the tablets on which the ten commandments were written. God gave Moses many other laws that governed ordinary life, feasts, and rites.

THE GOLDEN CALF

Meanwhile the people, seeing that Moses had not returned, said to
Aaron, "Now who will lead us? Let us give a face to God and make a
statue that we can see and touch." Then Aaron ordered that they
bring all the gold objects that they had. They melted them in a
fire and forged the image of a calf.

When the idol was raised on the altar, their doubts disappeared. They
cried out, "Behold, this is who brought us out of the land of Egypt!"
And they worshiped the calf. There were sacrifices, dances, and songs.
Thus, Moses found them when he descended from the mountain.

Seeing it going on, he became furious. He threw the tablets of the
law to the ground, smashed the idol, and severely punished the guilty.
They had not been able to resist even for a few days without a guide.
Moses felt sorry for their weakness and climbed the mountain again
to implore God's forgiveness.

The Lord said, "They are a stubborn people who forget my teachings,
but for your sake I will do as you ask. I will forgive them and lead
them to the promised land." God told Moses to carve the tablets of
the law again and renewed his covenant with Israel.

THE ARK OF THE COVENANT

When Moses returned to the camp he ordered an ark to be built to preserve the tablets of the law. The ark was a wooden box, all covered with gold, and two angels were carved on the lid. When the people of Israel were traveling, it was carried by the priests and nobody else could touch it. During the stops, when the people camped, the ark was kept in a tent called the tent of the covenant.

THE LAND OF CANAAN

The people of Israel resumed their march in the desert and finally arrived near the land of Canaan, the promised land. Moses sent twelve explorers, one from each tribe of Israel, to report on the peoples who inhabited it. After forty days the men came back full of fruit: pomegranates, figs, a huge bunch of grapes. Full of wonder, they reported on a land where "milk and honey flowed," just as the ancient stories said. But they also said, "Our enemies are powerful. They live in cities surrounded by high walls. We'll never be able to defeat them!" Among them, only Caleb and Joshua were confident: "We must not be afraid, the Lord is with us. We will conquer their cities!" But they were not heard. Frightened, the Israelites began to complain to each other: "Why did the Lord bring us here to make us die? Let us choose a new leader and let's go back to Egypt!"

The Lord became angry and said, "When will this people stop disrespecting me? All those who did not believe in me, despite having seen my miracles, will not enter the land I promised to their fathers."

The Israelites wandered for forty years in the desert
until all those who had not trusted the Lord died.
The Israelites never forgot what had happened to their
fathers and told their children and their children's children
about the miracles, the Israelites' unfaithfulness, the punishments,
and how the Lord had forgiven them every time.
When they reached the boundaries of the promised land, Moses
was now very old and felt he was nearing his end. He named Joshua,
who had always been faithful to God, as his successor.
"Be strong and do not be afraid," he told him. "The Lord walks
before you and will not abandon you."
Then he ascended Mount Nebo. From there, he looked at the
promised land for a long time, thanked the Lord for the immense
favors he had received, and fell asleep in the peace of the righteous.
After Moses' death, there was no other man to whom the Lord
spoke face-to-face.

JOSHUA THE LEADER

God said to Joshua, "You will lead the children of Israel to the land
I promised them. If you trust me, you will defeat every enemy."
Joshua prepared to cross the Jordan River and conquer the land of
Canaan. He ordered everyone to stock up on food and get ready,
then he called two men and instructed them to sneak into the first
city they would find on their way.

It was the fortress of Jericho, surrounded by high and well
defended walls.

The two spies in the city arrived at night and took refuge in a bad
neighborhood, in the house of a woman named Rahab. The arrival
of the two foreigners made the king of Jericho suspicious, and he
sent his soldiers to arrest them. Rahab hid the spies on her
terrace and told the soldiers, "They have already left. Perhaps
if you pursue them, you still have time to catch them."

After the soldiers had gone away, she went to reassure the two:
"We know that your God has done great things and that the fate of
this city is sealed. Swear to me that when you conquer it, you will
treat me and my family well." They swore and gave the woman a red
ribbon to put in the window of her house, as a sign of identification
during the battle. Then they fled, descending from a rope down
the walls.

Back in the camp, the spies said to Joshua, "The inhabitants of
Jericho already tremble knowing that we are approaching." Joshua
then gave everyone the order to head out. Arriving on the bank of
the Jordan, he told the priests, "Take the ark of the covenant and
walk before the people."

The Jordan was overflowing its banks, but as
soon as the priests entered the river with the
ark, the Red Sea miracle was repeated:
the waters parted, and the long column
of the Israelites crossed the dry riverbed.
It was Passover and the Jews celebrated it
on the plain outside of Jericho.

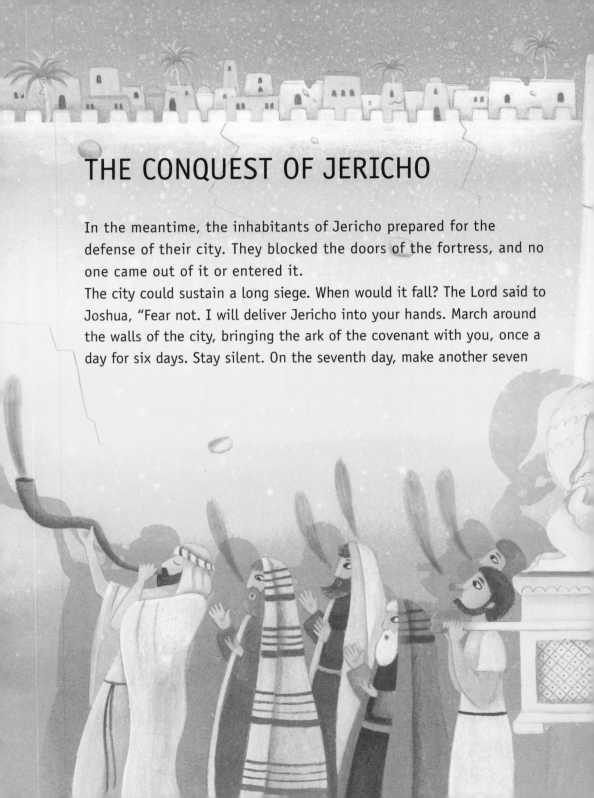

THE CONQUEST OF JERICHO

In the meantime, the inhabitants of Jericho prepared for the defense of their city. They blocked the doors of the fortress, and no one came out of it or entered it.

The city could sustain a long siege. When would it fall? The Lord said to Joshua, "Fear not. I will deliver Jericho into your hands. March around the walls of the city, bringing the ark of the covenant with you, once a day for six days. Stay silent. On the seventh day, make another seven

rounds around the walls, while the priests will sound the trumpets. Then the people shall let out a great war cry and the walls will fall." And that is what they did. On the seventh day, after the seventh circle around the city, Joshua said to the people, "Shout, for the Lord gives you the city!" At their shout the walls collapsed from the foundations and the Israelites entered the city. Jericho was destroyed and, according to the promise, only Rahab's house was spared because she recognized the power of the Lord.

IN THE PROMISED LAND

After the fall of Jericho, at the command of Joshua the army of Israel continued its victorious advance in the promised land by conquering other cities.

A great fear spread among the kings of the land of Canaan, who decided to ally themselves to defeat these new invaders.

But the Lord said to Joshua, "Do not be afraid. Nobody will resist before you."

A battle broke out outside the city of Gibeon. The army of Israel was about to win, but as sunset approached, Joshua knew the darkness of night could favor the enemies. "Sun, stand still!" shouted Joshua. And, miraculously, the light of that day lasted until complete victory. Thus, little by little, the Jews came into possession of the land that God had promised them. Joshua, according to the Lord's will, assigned to each of the twelve tribes a piece of the conquered territory.

Joshua could now step down, letting every tribe rule itself. When he felt near death, he gathered together the people he had bravely led and, with a solemn oath, made them renew their promise to serve the one true God.

The people swore, "We will serve the Lord our God and we will not abandon him to serve other gods." Joshua died and was buried in the mountains of Ephraim.

THE JUDGES

After the death of Joshua, every tribe of Israel lived in its territory without a leader to keep all the people united. Thus, over time, the Israelites forgot the oath made to the Lord and the laws that Moses had given them. They raised statues to the god Baal and worshiped foreign idols. When it happened, the Lord let them fall into the hands of the many enemies who were pressing on the borders of their lands.

But when Israel repented and asked for forgiveness, God gave strength and courage to people of faith called "judges," to save and free his people.

Among the many judges, two of them were Gideon and Samson. One of them was a woman, Deborah, who saved Israel not by force of arms, but by the power of wise advice.

GIDEON

One day the Lord spoke to Gideon, a peasant, and said to him, "Go and free Israel from the Midianites." But Gideon said, "Lord, I am not strong and brave. My family is poor, and I am the youngest of them all." The Lord replied, "Do not be afraid. I will be with you, and you will defeat the Midianites as if they were only one man." Then Gideon gathered an army of thirty-two thousand men. The Lord said, "You have too many people with you: I want to show Israel that victory depends only on my help. Order the fearful ones to go back home." Twenty-two thousand men went back. "They are still too many. Lead them to a spring. Those who lap the water with their tongues, as a dog laps, put them on one side, and then, on the other, put those who kneel down to drink by putting their hands to their mouths." Gideon obeyed, and the Lord said, "With the three hundred men who lapped, I will free you from the Midianites." The Midianite army was camped nearby. Gideon was cunning. When the night came, he gave each of the three hundred men a trumpet and an empty jar in which a lit torch had been placed. He told them, "Do what you will see me do!" After surrounding the enemy's camp, at Gideon's command, they blew the trumpets, broke the jars, and raised the torches, shouting together. The Midianites woke with a start and thought they had been attacked by a great army. Panicking, they fought blindly among themselves and finally fled in disarray. After this extraordinary victory, the Israelites wanted to make Gideon their king. But Gideon replied, "I will not be your king. Only the Lord will rule over you!" And he retired to his city.

SAMSON

After Gideon's death, many other judges led Israel. But the Israelites returned to worshipping idols, and the Lord, to punish them, made them fall for forty years under the power of the Philistines, who were warriors who came from the sea.

Once again, the Lord sent a judge to free them. His birth was announced to his parents by an angel: "You will consecrate him to God and his hair will never have to be cut." The child was called Samson, and he grew tall and strong.

His incredible strength soon made him famous, but no one knew the secret of his power. One day, in the countryside, he was attacked by a lion. Samson grabbed the lion and killed it with his bare hands.

Samson fell in love with a Philistine woman and married her. But that marriage was immediately a cause of conflicts and his

father-in-law forced his daughter to marry another man. Samson,
furious, set fire to the Philistine fields ready for harvest. For
revenge, the Philistines killed Samson's wife and her father.
From that moment on, there was war between Samson and
the Philistines.

The Philistines wanted to capture Samson, and the Israelites,
terrified by the threats of the rulers, begged him to give himself
up as their prisoner. Samson agreed, but when the Philistines were
about to take him, he broke the ropes that bound him, grabbed
the jawbone of a donkey, and used it to kill more than a thousand
enemies and then fled.

Samson then fell in love again with a Philistine woman, Delilah.
She loved only money, and so the Philistine leaders said to her,
"Find out where his strength comes from and we will cover you with
riches." Delilah went to work and tried in every way to find out
Samson's secret. Three times Samson had fun inventing imaginative
answers, but in the end, he opened his heart to her: "My strength

is in my hair. I have never been shaved because I am consecrated to God. If I cut my hair, I will lose my strength."

While Samson slept, Delilah ordered a man to shave his head, then she shouted, "Samson, the Philistines are coming for you! Wake up!" Samson woke up and thought, "I'll be able to escape as usual. They will not capture me!"

He did not realize that the Lord had abandoned him. The Philistines chained him, blinded him, and set him to turn the mill like a donkey. Time passed, and Samson's hair began to grow again.

One day the Philistine princes wanted to give a big party in honor of the god Dagon to thank him for the capture of their most dangerous enemy. The temple was filled with people, and to increase the fun they called Samson and forced him to play the fool for them. When at last he was brought among the pillars on which the temple rested, Samson pretended to want to rest and, to himself, prayed: "Lord, remember me. Give me strength this last time!" With his hands he found the two middle pillars on which the house stood, stretched out his arms, pushed hard against them, and he cried, "Let me die with the Philistines."

The temple collapsed, burying everyone under the rubble. Dying, Samson killed more enemies than in his whole life.

RUTH THE MOABITE

In the time when the people of Israel were governed by the judges, there was a tremendous famine and many Israelites emigrated. Elimelech of Bethlehem also left with his wife Naomi and their sons to the region of Moab, beyond the Jordan.

Years passed, and Elimelech died. His sons, who had married local women, died, too. So Elimelech's widow Naomi and her two daughters-in-law, Orpah and Ruth, were alone. Naomi missed her distant homeland, and when she learned that the famine there was over, she set off for Bethlehem with her daughters-in-law.

Along the way, Naomi thought, "Is it right for these two women to come with me?" Then she told them, "Go back to your mother's house. You have been good to me. May the Lord grant you to find security and a new husband." Crying, she kissed them one after the other. Orpah went away, but Ruth wanted to follow Naomi. She said, "Do not make me leave you! Wherever you go, I will come too. Your people will be mine, and your God will be my God."

Naomi and Ruth came to Bethlehem at the time of the barley harvest.
"If you allow it," said Ruth to Naomi, "I will go into the fields to
gather the ears of grain that have escaped the reapers' hands, so we
will be able to feed ourselves." And by chance she went to the field
of Boaz, a distant relative of Elimelech.

When he saw her, Boaz wanted to know who the young stranger was.
"She is Naomi's daughter-in-law, who came with her from the region
of Moab," they told him. Struck by Ruth's goodness and beauty, he
invited her not to go to other fields. He ordered his reapers to treat
her with respect and to let the ears fall on purpose so that Ruth
could gather them in abundance.

When Naomi heard of it, she was very happy and encouraged her
daughter-in-law to return to Boaz's field. At the end of the harvest,
Boaz realized that he loved Ruth and asked her to marry him.
The law allowed it, and everyone congratulated them.

And the day came when the news spread in Bethlehem: "A son was
born to Ruth!" Naomi was happy with that birth after so much pain.
The child was called Obed. From him was born Jesse, the father of
David, the great king of Israel.

SAMUEL IS CALLED BY GOD

A married couple went every year on a pilgrimage to the sanctuary
of Shiloh, where the ark of the covenant was kept.
The woman was very sad because she had no children and, crying,
she prayed, "Lord, do not forget me. If you give me the child
I desire, I will consecrate him to you." Eli, the priest of the
sanctuary, seeing her so grieved, consoled her, saying, "Go in peace.
The God of our fathers will listen to your prayer."
The following year the parents held the long-awaited baby in their
arms. They called him Samuel. When he was raised, according to
the woman's promise, they took him to the sanctuary and entrusted
him to Eli. The old priest, who had two greedy and wicked sons who
caused so much trouble for him, became very fond of little Samuel.
One night, while he slept in the temple of the Lord, Samuel woke up
with a start. Someone was calling him, "Samuel, Samuel!"
"Here I am!" he answered and ran to Eli. "You called me?"
"No, my son, go back to sleep," Eli told him.
But the voice called again, "Samuel!" And again, Samuel ran to Eli.
"I did not call you. Go back to sleep," Eli said.
When the voice awoke Samuel for the third time, Eli said to the boy,
"If you hear this call again, answer, 'Speak, Lord, your servant is
listening to you.'"
The voice called, and Samuel replied, "Speak, Lord, your servant is
listening to you." Then God spoke to him: "In Israel, terrible things
will happen. Eli's children will die and he, too, will die because he
has not punished his children for the evil they have done." At dawn,
Samuel was sad for his old teacher, and when he told him the message,

Eli said with resignation, "Do whatever God wants! He is right."
The Philistines waged war on the Israelites and defeated them,
killing them by the thousands, including Eli's two sons. When Eli
found out, he died of pain.
Years passed, and Samuel was made a judge of Israel. Under his
leadership, the people returned to serving the Lord again and
defeated their enemies.

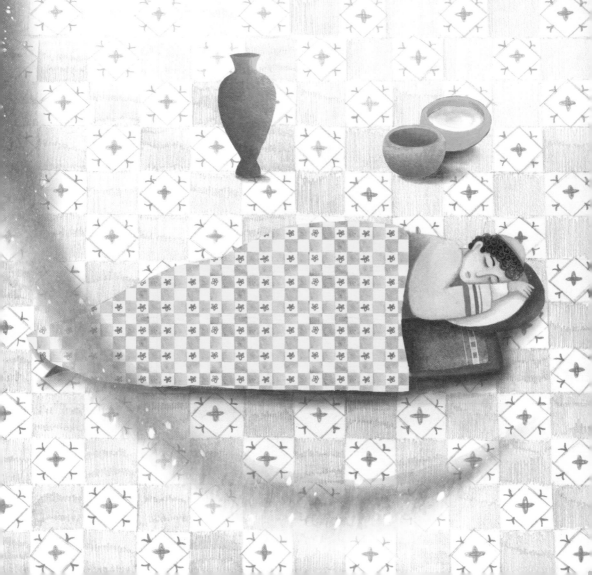

THE FIRST KING

Samuel was loved by all but, when he grew old, the Israelites, fearing to remain without a leader, asked him, "Give us a king to govern us, as all other nations have." Samuel was angry, because only God could be king of Israel, but they insisted.

The Lord said, "Listen to them. They do not trust me. Give them a king. I'll show you the man I chose." The next day Samuel met Saul of the tribe of Benjamin, and God said, "Behold the king. It is him." So Samuel anointed Saul's head with oil, a symbol of God's power and strength, to wisely govern and defend Israel from its enemies.

Saul won many battles and ruled for a few years with courage and goodness, but over time he became prideful and wanted to do as it pleased him. Samuel reproached him several times, but the king did not listen to him.

DAVID THE SHEPHERD

Samuel was sad for Saul, but the Lord said to him, "Stop thinking about Saul. He will no longer reign over Israel. Fill your horn with oil and go to Jesse in Bethlehem, because I have chosen a king among his sons."

Samuel went secretly to the house of Jesse, examined his children one by one, asking, "Lord, is your chosen one of these?"

"Do not mind their appearance or height. I look at the heart. My chosen one is not among these!" answered God.

So Samuel asked Jesse, "Are all your children here?"

"There is one missing, the youngest; he is keeping the sheep," replied the father. They went to call him and, when the boy arrived, the voice of God said to Samuel, "It's him." Samuel anointed him, and from that moment the Spirit of the Lord was upon David.

Saul continued to reign, but the Lord had abandoned him, and Samuel no longer spoke to him. The king felt increasingly sad and upset and often made terrible scenes. "Perhaps music could distract him," thought his servants and learned that David was a skilled harpist. The young shepherd was called to court and, when the king sank into anger or melancholy, David played the harp and sang for him. In those moments, peace returned to the heart of the king and Saul ended up becoming attached to the boy.

THE DEFEAT OF THE GIANT GOLIATH

The war with the Philistines resumed once again. Goliath—a giant Philistine warrior—launched a challenge: "Choose one man who will fight with me. If he kills me, then all the Philistines will be your slaves!" Every day he appeared before the Israel's camp and repeated these words, but no one had the courage to face him, not even Saul. When David heard the giant's challenge, he came to Saul and said, "I will go and fight him!"

"You cannot! You're too young and you're not a warrior," said the king. "The Lord gave me the strength to face and kill the lions and bears that attacked my flock. He will also save me from this Philistine." Saul, moved by these words, gave David his own armor to wear. But the helmet and the bronze breastplate were too big for him and he was not used to them. So he took them off and, armed only with a shepherd's staff and a slingshot, went to the stream, picked up five well-polished stones, then went to face the enemy.

When Goliath saw David before him, he laughed at him and came forward confidently. Immediately David put a stone in his sling and threw it. It happened in a moment: the stone struck Goliath in the forehead so powerfully that he fell to the ground. David stood over Goliath, pulled his sword from his side, and cut off his head with it. The Philistines, seeing their gigantic champion die, fled, pursued by the Israelites.

The news of David's victory spread in a flash. The women came out of their homes in all the cities of Israel dancing and singing, "Saul, the great king, has killed a thousand, but David ten thousand!" When he heard that song, Saul became angry, saying "What does this mean? All that's left is for them to make David king in my place."

SAUL'S DEATH

Everyone looked at David with affection and admiration. Even
Saul's son Jonathan became his friend, and Michal, Saul's younger
daughter, fell in love with him. Saul became increasingly jealous
of David and came to hate him so much that he showed it openly.

One day, in a moment of anger, he threw a spear at David, who was singing for him, and later tried several times to get him killed, pushing him to carry out dangerous tasks. David understood that near Saul his life would always be in danger, so he took refuge in the desert with a small army of faithful companions. For years Saul chased him, and David continued to escape but never tried to take revenge. One day, during a chase, Saul went into a cave alone, without realizing that David was with him in the darkness. Unknown to Saul, David cut off the edge of Saul's cloak, and after the king had left the cave and started away with his soldiers, David called out him waving the piece of his cloak in his hand. "Why do you persecute me?" he said. "Look! I could have killed you, but I took pity on you. I will never raise my hand against my king. May the Lord judge between you and me!" Saul, seeing him, wept and understood that David was a better man than he was and that the Lord would give him his kingdom.

Despite this he continued to hunt David. In the meantime, Samuel died and all of Israel wept for him because a great prophet had been lost.

The Philistines resumed the war and during a battle they killed the king's son Jonathan, and then wounded Saul. The king, fearing to end up in the hands of his enemies, threw himself on his own sword and died.

When a messenger announced the death of Saul and his friend Jonathan, David burst into tears and composed in their honor a beautiful song.

DAVID, KING OF ISRAEL

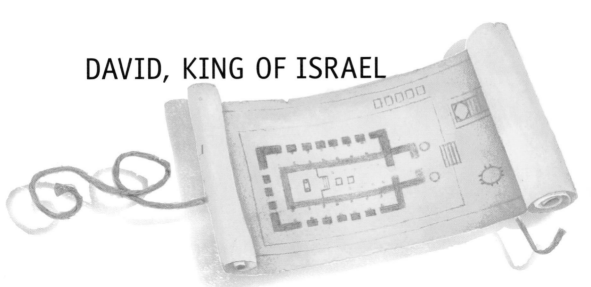

After the death of Saul, David was recognized as king of all the tribes of Israel. During his reign Israel's enemies were gradually defeated and the kings of the neighboring peoples sent him ambassadors with rich gifts as a sign of friendship. David conquered Jerusalem, making it the capital of the kingdom, and then transferred the ark of the covenant, a sign of the presence of God, to the city. A festive procession accompanied the ark carried by the priests. The king himself led the way by dancing and the people praised the Lord to the sound of the trumpets.

But David felt like he had not done enough for the Lord who had always been good to him. So he sent for the prophet Nathan and said, "I live in a splendid palace and the Lord lives in a tent! I want to build a temple for the ark." That same night the Lord spoke to Nathan, saying, "Say to my servant David: 'I do not want a house, but I want to be a house for him! I made him a great king, but he will not build me a temple. His son will do it. But I promise him that his descendants and his kingdom will be steadfast forever. If he does evil I will punish him, but I will never stop loving him.'"

All the people admired and loved David for his goodness. But, as we know, persevering in being good is very difficult. A sunny afternoon, while his soldiers were at war, from the terrace of the palace David saw a beautiful woman who was bathing. It was Bathsheba, the wife of Uriah, a general of his army. David wanted her for himself and, to carry out his plan, he sent Uriah to the battlefront, so he could die in battle.

David then took Bathsheba as a wife and had a son with her. But what David had done was bad. The Lord sent the prophet Nathan to tell the king this story: "There were two men, one rich and the other poor. The rich man had many sheep and oxen, while the poor man had only one sheep. A guest came to the house of the rich man, and to prepare a banquet, the rich man took the poor man's only sheep and killed it."

"Tell me, who is this man! He deserves to be punished," cried David. And the prophet said, "That man is you."

David recognized his guilt and asked for forgiveness: "Have mercy on me, O God, in your great mercy. In your immense goodness, erase my sin. Wash me and I will become whiter than snow."

Sadly, David and Bathsheba's child died. After some time, they had another child whom they called Solomon, whom the Lord loved very much.

ABSALOM'S REBELLION

The Lord forgave David, but after that his family was the cause of many troubles. Among his many children, born of different wives, jealousies and rivalries were unleashed that their father could do nothing to prevent. David's son Absalom hated his brother Amnon so much that, one day, during a banquet he ordered his servants to kill him, and they did.

How could he face his father after killing Amnon, his favorite son, the heir to the throne? Absalom fled far to avoid the king's punishment. But he was still his son and, after three years of exile, David wanted to make peace with him. The king's heart was sincere, but Absalom became prideful and only wanted to take his father's place.

Handsome, with long hair that fell over his shoulders, Absalom rode around the city of Jerusalem on his chariot, causing problems and inciting its people against David. "The king does not listen to you. If I were in his place, I could rule with justice," he said. When he thought he had the people on his side, he openly rebelled, took charge of an army, and had himself proclaimed king. David was saddened by the betrayal of his son, but to avoid a war with him, he left Jerusalem on foot, followed by all the people who remained loyal to him. The palace and the city were empty and Absalom entered without a fight. But later David's army fought Absalom's, and the rebels were defeated. As Absalom fled through a forest on the back of a mule, his long hair, of which he was so proud, got tangled in the branches of a tree and David's soldiers found him hanging from it. "Do not hurt Absalom," David had advised his generals before the battle. But thinking that the kingdom would

never be safe as long as Absalom remained alive, they killed him
mercilessly. At the news of his son's death, David wept so much that
he seemed more like the loser than the winner of the battle.
In the last years of his reign, David faced famine and pestilence,
but he remained faithful to the Lord.
Remembering the promise of the Lord, he named Solomon,
the son of Bathsheba, his successor, and then he died in peace.
He had reigned for forty years. He was the true founder of the
kingdom of Israel and made Jerusalem its political and religious
capital. He was not only a great king, but also a poet and a
musician. The prayers he composed are part of the book of Psalms
and we still pray them today because they speak to the hearts of
people and of God.

SOLOMON, A WISE KING

Solomon was only seventeen when he became king. He loved the Lord and the Lord loved Solomon in return. One night the Lord appeared to Solomon in a dream and said to him, "Ask whatever you want, and I will give it to you." "I am only a boy," replied Solomon. "How can I govern this people with justice in the place of my father? Grant me, please, a heart that knows how to distinguish good from evil." The Lord said, "Since you have not asked me for riches and glory,

I will not only grant you a wise and intelligent heart,
but also all that you have not asked for."
Solomon became a wise king, rich and powerful.
One day two mothers came to him and one of them said,
"Listen, my King, this woman and I live in the same house. We both
gave birth to a son. During the night her son died and while I was
sleeping, she took my baby and now she says it is hers. I want
my baby back."
"That's not true!" shouted the other one with the baby in her arms.
"This child is mine! Her son is the one who died!" And they
kept arguing.
With no witnesses, how could Solomon establish the truth?
He ordered, "Bring a sword, cut the child in two, and give each
woman half."
One of the two women, bursting into tears, cried out, "Do not kill
my child. Just give him to her!" The other instead said, "That is
right, the child should not be mine nor hers—cut it!"
Then Solomon said, "Give the child to the first woman
who spoke, because she is the real mother."

THE CONSTRUCTION OF THE TEMPLE

Thanks to Solomon's wise government, his people lived in
peace and prosperity. The king made agreements and alliances with
neighboring peoples and there were no more wars at the far ends of
the kingdom. Trade by land and sea brought great wealth to Israel.
It was Solomon who built the temple of Jerusalem.
Thousands and thousands of men were employed to carve the
precious cedar wood from the forests of Lebanon, to extract the
stone from the mountains, and prepare the large, square boulders of
the foundations. The king himself directed and supervised the work.
It took three years to prepare the materials and seven years to
build it, but when it was finished, the temple was a majestic
building, as they had never seen before. Only priests could enter
it and the people stood in the great courtyard where there was an
altar for offerings and a circular basin resting on twelve bronze
oxen for the water of the ablutions.
When the time came, Solomon brought the ark that contained the
tablets that God had delivered to Moses on Mount Horeb. Animal
sacrifices were made, and, with a solemn procession, the ark was
placed in the Holy of Holies, the most sacred and hidden room of
the whole temple.
When the priests had gone out, a cloud invaded the temple,
a sign that the Lord had taken possession of his house.
Then Solomon prayed, "Lord, listen to anyone who prays to you in
this place. And if a foreigner comes to pray, please answer
his prayers as well." Then he blessed the people and there was
a big party.

In the silence of the night, after the king was asleep, God appeared again to Solomon. God said, "I have heard your prayer and I have chosen this place as my house. My eyes will be open, my ears will be attentive to your prayers. But if you abandon my laws and serve other gods, I will take you from my land and abandon you."

THE QUEEN OF SHEBA

Solomon's fame had spread all over the world.
Even the Queen of Sheba had heard about the riches, wisdom,
and intelligence of the king of Israel and wanted to go and
get to know him. She left the Arabian peninsula, where her
kingdom was located, with a caravan of hundreds of elephants
and camels laden with gold, precious gems, and spices.

Solomon received her with all the honors and the queen was impressed by the beauty of Jerusalem and the temple. She admired the way the kingdom was administered and questioned Solomon about many things, and he answered all her questions, even the most difficult ones. Finally, the queen exclaimed, "It was true what I had heard of you. Blessed be the Lord your God who made you king!"

The two sovereigns exchanged magnificent gifts and the queen returned to her country.

THE DIVISION OF THE KINGDOM

Like the rulers of his time, and like his father David, Solomon had many wives. They were foreign women, daughters of powerful allied kings who, having come to Israel, had continued to offer sacrifices to their gods and built altars and temples.

These pagan cults had spread among the people and Solomon, who was now old and fragile, and despite his wisdom, assisted in these rites. The Lord said to Solomon, "Because you have not been faithful to me and have not followed my laws, I will snatch the kingdom from your descendants and give it to one of your servants. But out of respect to the promise made to your father David, I will let your son reign over Jerusalem."

After Solomon's death, the kingdom was split into two: the kingdom of Israel in the north, consisting of ten tribes and with Samaria as its capital, and the kingdom of Judah in the south, consisting of only two tribes and with Jerusalem as its capital. Many times again the people and their kings fell into the sin of idolatry by turning away from God. But the Lord sent prophets in both kingdoms, people who spoke in his name and taught his ways.

Samaria

THE PROPHET ELIJAH

When Ahab was king of Israel, God sent the prophet Elijah to proclaim, "For three years not a single drop of water will fall from heaven because you, king, have abandoned the law of the Lord and worshiped false gods."

Then Elijah found refuge in a cave. Here he fed on the food the crows, sent by the Lord, brought him morning and evening, and he quenched his thirst with the water of the nearby stream. Meanwhile, due to the lack of rain, a terrible famine struck the country and even the stream dried up. God then ordered Elijah to set out for the city of Zarephath. At the city's gates, Elijah met a widow who gathered wood, and he asked her for water and bread. "I have no bread, just a little flour and oil. I want to cook what's left for me and my son so that we may eat it, and then die," the woman replied. "Do not worry," said Elijah. "Go and bake some bread for me, too, and I assure you that you will not lack anything until the end of the famine."

The woman obeyed and so it happened: all three ate in abundance and the prophet remained a guest in their house in the following days, and the cupboard was never empty.

One day the widow's son became seriously ill and died. The woman was overwhelmed by grief, but Elijah began to pray, "Lord, this woman has been good to me. Give life back to her son." And her son came back to life.

Jerusalem

THE PRIESTS OF BAAL

After three years of drought Elijah went to King Ahab and challenged him, saying, "Gather all the people on Mount Carmel. Make two piles of wood, and on each the priests of the god Baal and I will offer sacrifices. Nobody will light the fire. The priests of Baal will invoke their god, and I will invoke the name of the Lord. We will know which one is the true God by the one who sends fire to consume the sacrifice." In front of the gathered people of Israel, the four hundred fifty priests of Baal began loudly shouting out their prayers. They shouted from dawn to noon, but nobody answered. Elijah made fun of them: "Shout louder, perhaps your god is deaf!" They started to shout even more, but not a spark came from the sky.

Then Elijah said, "O God of Israel, show that you are the true God so that everyone will know that I am your servant and that I do this in your name."

And behold, a fire came down from heaven and in an instant burned the wood and Elijah's sacrifice. All the people knelt and said, "The Lord is the true God!"

As they repented, the long-awaited rain arrived. Elijah saw it coming. He climbed to the top of Mount Carmel with a servant and began to pray. Then he ordered his servant, "Look toward the sea and tell me what you see." The servant said, "I see a small little cloud coming." "It is time for us to go," Elijah answered. "The rain is coming." Suddenly the wind blew, the sky became dark with clouds, and the rain began to pour down.

ELIJAH IN THE DESERT

The king was impressed by the miracles that Elijah performed, but his wife Queen Jezebel was furious at the defeat of the priests of Baal. So that he would not be killed, Elijah escaped to the desert. He was tired and discouraged, and he sat in the shade of a broom tree and begged the Lord to take his life. Then he fell asleep. While he was asleep, an angel touched him and said, "Get up and eat. A long journey awaits you."

Elijah woke up and found a jug of water and some bread beside him. He ate and drank, and that food gave him the strength to walk for forty days and forty nights to Mount Horeb.

There the voice of the Lord asked him, "Elijah, why are you here?"
Elijah answered, "Lord, I am alone; no one listens to me. Now they
want to kill me." The voice said, "I want to show myself to you." The
wind rushed, but the Lord was not in the wind. An earthquake came,
but the Lord was not in the earthquake. Fire fell from the sky, but the
Lord was not in the fire. Then there was the whisper of a light wind.
When Elijah heard it, he knew the Lord was there, so he covered his
face. The Lord said, "Go on your way. You will not be alone anymore.
There will be another man who is loyal to God, and you will have a
successor, named Elisha, who will be a prophet after you."

THE CHARIOT OF FIRE

Elijah did what the Lord had told him and went to Damascus. When he was still a long way off, he saw Elisha plowing a field.
Elijah went to him, and when he reached Elisha, he threw his cloak over him. Elisha realized he had been chosen by God. So he said goodbye to his father and mother and followed Elijah as his disciple.

When Elijah felt that his life was about to end, he headed for the
Jordan River. Elisha did not want to leave him and went with him.
When they reached the shore, Elijah struck the waters with his cloak
and the waters parted, allowing them to pass through. Suddenly, a
horse-drawn chariot of fire appeared and took Elijah to heaven.
Elisha, overcome with emotion, cried out, "Father, father, stay! You are
the guide of Israel!" But Elijah's cloak was all that remained of him.
Elisha picked up the cloak and returned. When he arrived at the Jordan,
he thought, "Will the waters part for me? Will I have Elijah's power?"
He touched the current of the river with the cloak, and the waters
parted. Not far away, some men of the city of Jericho who saw this
happen said, "The spirit of Elijah has rested on you. Be blessed, Elisha!"
Elisha became a great prophet. He performed many miracles and
helped the needy. He continued Elijah's work,
teaching the people and kings of Israel about
the love of the Lord God and his laws.

THE PROPHET HOSEA

Other prophets came to remind the people and kings of Israel that infidelity to God would lead to ruin, but fidelity to salvation and peace. Among others, there was Hosea, married to a woman who had betrayed him and that the prophet had forgiven and welcomed back. The story of Hosea was an example the Lord used to invite his people to come back to him, because his love was greater than infidelity. But every call was useless, and the announced catastrophe came true. The northern kingdom was defeated by the Assyrian army, and the city of Samaria was conquered and sacked after a long siege. The Assyrians enslaved the surviving population and dispersed it in the territories of their empire. And the deported tribes did not return.

THE PROPHET ISAIAH

Even in the small kingdom of Judah, in the south, the Lord chose
men who spoke in his name.

Isaiah was a noble and wise man. One day, while he was in the
temple, the Lord appeared to him on a throne suspended in the sky,
surrounded by angels; the hem of his robe filled the temple. Isaiah
was scared. "I am not worthy to stand before the Lord!" he cried
out. Then one of the angels took a charcoal from the temple altar,
flew toward Isaiah, and purified his lips.

Isaiah had been chosen as a prophet of God.

Isaiah announced that the kingdom of Judah would be swept away
by enemies, the city of Jerusalem would be destroyed, and the
people deported, just as had happened to the northern kingdom.
But his prophecies did not speak only of suffering and destruction;
they also announced the promise that God would not abandon his
people: "The Lord will do a new thing. Even now it is coming." He
said that a descendant of the house of David would come to restore
peace and justice on earth: "A child will come, he will be called
God the Almighty, Eternal Father, Prince of Peace."

THE PROPHET JEREMIAH

Another important prophet was Jeremiah. His family had a bad reputation, but the Lord called him saying, "I have always known you. Even before you were born I established that you would become my prophet." Jeremiah felt confused and said, "I cannot speak well, and I'm still too young!"

Then the Lord touched his mouth and said, "Behold, from now on you will speak in my name, and I will not forsake you."

Then he asked Jeremiah, "What do you see?"

"I see a branch of an almond tree," he replied.

And the Lord said, "It is the sign that I watch over my word to make it happen. Go and announce to the inhabitants of Jerusalem that I am going to abandon them into the hands of their enemies, because they have become wicked and have forgotten me. But if they recognize their faults and return to me, I will save them and protect them."

Jeremiah did what the Lord had commanded him, but instead of repenting, his fellow citizens made fun of him and persecuted him.

And so the kingdom of Judah was attacked by the Babylonian army. The temple that King Solomon had built was set on fire, and the city of Jerusalem was reduced to a mass of ruins.

The people who survived the massacres were deported to Babylon, and only a few peasants continued to live in Judea. But Jeremiah comforted them. The promise God had made to David would be kept. The prisoners would return from exile, and the Lord would establish with his people a new covenant, written not on stone tablets but in their hearts.

TOBIT AND HIS SON TOBIAH

Tobit lived in Nineveh with his wife Anna and son Tobiah. He was one of the many Jews who had ended up in exile, but even here he remained faithful to the law of the Lord. Tobit consoled and encouraged other exiles and shared what he had with the poor. And despite being strictly forbidden, he secretly buried the abandoned bodies of murdered Israelites. One day he fell ill and became blind. "See what has become of you! What good did all your good deeds do you?" his wife scolded him. Even the neighbors made fun of him. Tobit was grieved, but he endured everything patiently. He was old and felt close to death. Then he remembered something. He called his son Tobiah and said to him, "Go to Media, in the city of Rages, to our relative Gabael, to take back the money I deposited with him. The journey is long, so find someone whom you can trust to go with you." When Tobiah went in search of a traveling companion, the Lord sent the angel Raphael to him. He looked like a young man and said he knew the way to Media.

Tobiah did not know that he was in company of an angel. He only knew that the man seemed trustworthy. They packed their bags, said goodbye to Anna and Tobit, and left accompanied by a dog.

In the evening, they came by the River Tigris. While Tobiah was washing his feet, suddenly a big fish came out of the water, trying to bite him. Quickly they grabbed it, and Raphael said, "Open the fish. Remove the gall, the heart, and the liver, and store them. You will need them." They roasted the rest of the fish for dinner.

During the journey they saw the city of Ecbatana from afar, and Raphael said to Tobiah, "There lives Raguel, a relative of yours, with his daughter Sarah. She is beautiful and smart. Why not ask if you can marry her?"

Tobiah answered, "I heard about her. She has already had seven husbands. They all died on the evening of the wedding because a jealous demon does not allow anybody to approach her."

"Do not worry about this demon and marry her," Raphael said. "God has destined her for you from eternity. You will save her."

From that moment Tobiah could not wait to meet Sarah. When they arrived at Ecbatana, they introduced themselves to her father and Tobiah asked to marry her. Raguel consented but feared that again this time the marriage would end in tragedy. After the wedding banquet, Tobiah and Sarah retreated to their room and closed the door.

Tobiah, at the suggestion of Raphael, took the heart and the liver of the fish from his sack and threw them into the burning brazier. The smell of the fish made the demon flee, who found himself chained by the hand of Raphael and thrown into the realm of darkness. In the morning the servants found Tobiah and Sarah quietly asleep in their bed.

There were many days of celebration, and in the meantime, Raphael went to collect the money on behalf of Tobiah.

It was time to get back on the road to Nineveh, where Tobiah's parents waited for their son anxiously.

The dog, who had accompanied Raphael and Tobiah on the journey, followed them. When they got back home, Raphael ordered Tobiah: "Take the gall of the fish and spread it on your father's eyes."

Tobiah obeyed, and old Tobit regained his sight. In tears Tobit hugged Sarah and welcomed her into his house.

When Tobit and Tobiah wanted to reward Raphael for all he had done, the angel revealed himself to them, saying, "The Lord saw the pain of Tobit and Sarah and sent me to heal them. Bless God and tell everyone what he has done for you." And he disappeared from their sight.

JONAH

Nineveh was the capital of the Assyrians, who had defeated
and deported the people of Israel and made them slaves.
One day the Lord ordered the prophet Jonah, "Go to
Nineveh, the great city, and tell its inhabitants that they
must repent of their wickedness or I will punish them." But
Jonah did not agree. If the people of Nineveh had committed evil,
too bad for them. He hoped the Lord would punish them! Instead of
doing as God asked, he fled in the opposite direction and got on a ship.
Then the Lord unleashed a storm on the sea like no one had ever
seen before. The terrified sailors each prayed to their god and threw
things overboard into the sea to try to lighten the ship and keep it
from sinking, but it was useless. Meanwhile, Jonah hid in a corner of
the hold of the ship. The captain of the ship said, "Maybe someone
among us is responsible for all this. Let's cast lots to find out who
he is." They cast lots and the lot fell on Jonah. Jonah understood
what was happening and admitted, "It is because of me that the
storm broke out. I am an Israelite. My God is the Lord who made
heaven and earth, and I escaped from him."
"What should we do with you?" they asked him.
"Throw me into the sea, and the storm will calm down," Jonah said.
The sailors prayed to the Lord, saying, "Do not punish us if we are
forced to kill him." Then they took Jonah and threw him into the
waves. Immediately the sea returned quiet.
But Jonah did not die. The Lord sent a large fish to swallow him up. For
three days and three nights, Jonah lived in the belly of the fish, praying
in the darkness. After three days the fish threw him back onto the beach.

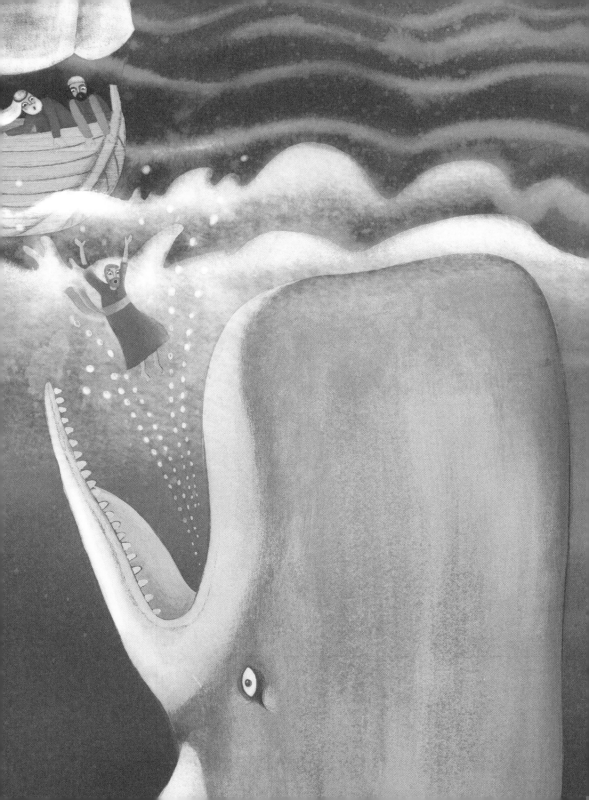

The Lord said to Jonah again, "Go to Nineveh and speak in my name." This time Jonah obeyed. He walked the length and breadth of the city, shouting aloud, "In forty days the city will be destroyed." The people of Nineveh, old and young, believed Jonah, they put on sackcloth and stopped eating and drinking. The king also stripped off his robe and ordered that everyone in his kingdom should do penance, both people and animals, saying, "Everyone should repent of their bad deeds and the evil they have committed. Ask the Lord with all your heart to change his mind and not let us die." The Lord saw their goodwill and forgave them.

But Jonah was angry. He said to the Lord, "Why did you bring me here? I knew it would end this way! You are good to everyone and you are moved to forgive."

The Lord replied, "Do you think it is right what you are saying?" Jonah did not answer. He went into the desert where he built a shelter and from there he looked at Nineveh. Maybe the Lord would change his mind; perhaps he would destroy the city anyway.

The Lord made a bush grow up over Jonah. It was very hot, and Jonah was happy with the cool shade that the bush provided; gradually his anger cooled down. But the next day a worm ate the roots of the plant and a wind dried it up. The sun beat down harshly on his head and Jonah felt faint. Immediately he began to complain: "I want to die."

"Does it seem right to be angry because a bush died?" the Lord asked.

"Yes, I think it's right," Jonah answered stubbornly.

The Lord scolded him, "If you feel sorry for the plant that you did not plant or grow, why should I not have mercy on Nineveh, where so many of my creatures live?"

And Jonah said nothing more.

JUDITH

Even in the most difficult periods, there were among the people of
Israel men and women faithful to the Lord who knew how to instill
courage and trust in their brothers and sisters. During their exile,
the Israelites loved to tell their stories. One of these was about
a woman named Judith. At the time of King Nebuchadnezzar, the
Babylonian general Holofernes besieged the small town of Bethulia.
Holofernes was a cruel man, and the people of the city knew what
happened to those who tried to fight back. All the water supplies
were cut off and the besieged people wanted to give in.

Judith lived in Bethulia. She was a young woman, a widow and childless, but she had faith in the Lord and did not want to surrender. She decided to act alone. After praying, she wore her most beautiful dress and beautiful jewels. She took some food and walked with a servant toward the enemy camp.

When the Babylonian soldiers saw her, they were amazed at her beauty and asked her what she wanted. "I do not want to die with the others. I escaped from the city and I can give your commander secure information to conquer it." The guards led her to Holofernes's tent. The general, enchanted by the charm of Judith, believed every word and wanted to give a feast in her honor. That night Holofernes drank so much wine that he got drunk, and when his servants left them alone, he fell into a deep sleep. Judith acted quickly. She sent her servant out of the tent, then picked up Holofernes's heavy sword, grabbed him by the hair, and struck his neck twice, cutting off his head. The maid wrapped his head in a cloth and hid it in her food bag. Then the two women left the camp without the guards suspecting anything.

The next morning Holofernes's head hung from the wall of Bethulia. When the enemy soldiers saw his head, they fled in terror, abandoning the siege.

DANIEL

Another story was about a young man named Daniel and three of his friends.

Nebuchadnezzar, the great king of Babylon, had brought them to his court to be educated in the language of the Chaldeans and enter his service. The Lord helped the four young men to learn many things, especially Daniel who could interpret dreams and visions.

One night, Nebuchadnezzar had a bad dream, and the next morning he immediately summoned the wise men and fortune-tellers to explain it to him. They all waited to hear what the king would say about his dream, but the king got mad and said, "What sort of soothsayers are you? If you cannot even guess my dream, how on earth are you going to interpret it?" And he threatened to condemn them to death. When Daniel learned of it, he asked to be received at court.

The Lord told Daniel to say: "O king, you have seen in a dream a great statue. It had a golden head, a chest and arms of silver, a belly and thighs of bronze, legs of iron, and feet of clay. A stone, falling from a mountain, hit its clay feet and the whole statue was shattered. Then the stone became a mountain so big it filled the earth."

Nebuchadnezzar was amazed; that was his dream.

Daniel continued, "The golden head is you, O king; God has granted you strength and glory. The other metals are the kingdoms that will come after yours, some stronger, others weaker. But eventually a new kingdom will come, the kingdom of God, which will destroy the previous ones and last forever."

Nebuchadnezzar said, "Your God is the greatest of all, and he also knows the mysteries of the future." Then he appointed Daniel governor of Babylon and his friends as administrators.

THE THREE YOUNG MEN IN THE FIERY FURNACE

One day, Nebuchadnezzar built a huge golden statue to show everyone his power, and he ordered, "Whenever my subjects hear music, they will have to kneel and worship the statue.

Whoever will not do it will be thrown into a fiery furnace."
Daniel's friends, Hananiah, Mishael, and Azariah, refused to
worship the statue. Brought before the king, they said, "We
worship only the Lord God. Know, O king, that if he wants he
can save us from the fire of the furnace. But even if the Lord
does not save us, we will never serve other gods."
The king was furious. These young men, whom the king had filled
with honors and made his administrators, refused to kneel before
his statue? He immediately ordered them to be tied and thrown
into the furnace where the flames rose very high.
But an angel of the Lord came to block the flames surrounding
Hananiah, Mishael, and Azariah with a wind full of dew. The
king, amazed by what he saw, heard a song of praise coming
from the furnace and, when he looked again, he saw them
walking in the fire.
Then he cried out, "Servants of the Lord God, come out."
The three came out of the flames without even a burn and
Nebuchadnezzar said, "Blessed be your God to whom you remained
faithful at the cost of your lives. He is truly the Lord of all."

DANIEL IN THE LIONS' DEN

After Nebuchadnezzar's death, his empire was taken over by the Persian king Darius. The new king appreciated the intelligence and wisdom of Daniel and appointed him governor.

The other court officials, however, were jealous of Daniel and tried to make him look bad. Eventually they figured out a way to get rid of him. They went to the king and said, "Tell your subjects to bow only before you and no other god. Anyone who will not obey will be thrown into the lions' den." They knew that Daniel would never obey.

The king thought this was a good idea and he signed the decree. Daniel ignored the decree and continued to pray as usual, kneeling before the Lord three times a day. It was easy for his enemies to accuse him of disobedience. When the king heard of it, he was sorry because he loved Daniel and tried in every way to save him, but the law is the law. In the end, he ordered him to be thrown to the lions. And when a large stone closed the mouth of the pit, Darius could only say, "May that God whom you serve so faithfully save you!"

The king did not sleep all night. The next morning, he hurried to the den, called to Daniel, and with great joy he heard him reply, "I'm fine! The Lord sent an angel to shut the lions' mouths because I did no harm to him or to you."

The king ordered that Daniel be freed immediately and that his accusers be thrown into the den.

As soon as the lions saw them, they rushed and ate them.

QUEEN ESTHER

The story of Esther also became famous, passing from one generation to another.

One day in the city of Susa, the Persian King Ahasuerus gave a great feast. He wanted to show off the beauty of his wife Queen Vashti. But the queen did not show up. The offended king made her pay for her disobedience. He said he never wanted to see her again and gave orders that the most beautiful girls be brought to court from all over the kingdom. From among these he would choose his new queen. Among them was Esther, the cousin of a man named Mordecai, a Jew who, thanks to his honesty and abilities, had become a court official. Mordecai was very fond of his cousin and advised her to keep her origins secret. When Ahasuerus saw Esther, he immediately fell in love with her and chose her as his wife.

Meanwhile, at court, Mordecai had made an enemy: the powerful minister Haman. Everyone was afraid of him and knelt before him, except for Mordecai who knelt only before the Lord. To take revenge, Haman accused Mordecai and the Jews of being rebels. Ahasuerus believed his words and ordered that all the Jews of the kingdom be killed, setting the date of the massacre. Mordecai was desperate and shouted, "A people that did nothing wrong is destroyed!" He sent a message to Esther saying, "Only you can save us. Maybe you have become queen for this. Go to the king and speak in our favor." Esther knew that no one could approach the king without an invitation, not even the queen, on pain of death. But she decided to try.

She asked all the Jews to pray and fast with her for three days. At the end of the three days, she put on her most beautiful dress and, accompanied by her maidservants, presented herself before the king. She was beautiful and smiled, but her heart pounded with fear.

When Ahasuerus, who was very angry, looked at her, Esther paled and felt faint. Then the king softened and laid his scepter upon her as a sign of forgiveness, and said, "What do you wish, Esther? Whatever you ask me, I will grant you."

The queen replied, "If you want to make me happy, come with Haman to the banquet I have prepared."

At the end of the feast, Ahasuerus repeated his question, and this time Esther replied, "My king, I beg you to grant life to me and my people. We have been condemned to destruction because

of a dishonest man who is not worthy to live in your palace."
"Tell me who this man is and I will do justice," said the king.
"It's him," Esther said, pointing to Haman.
The king realized that he had been deceived. He ordered Haman
to be arrested and had him killed on a stake he had prepared for
Mordecai. Then he canceled the order to kill the Jewish people
and appointed Mordecai as minister.
The Jews still remember Queen Esther and the danger they escaped
each year on the feast of Purim.

THE SILENT HARPS

The stories we have read so far kept alive the people's faith in a better tomorrow during the sad period of exile. At first the Jews were treated as slaves. Then, little by little, their living conditions improved, and they were allowed to meet in villages. Some of them even made a career and entered the service of foreign kings.

But the bitterness of having lost their country was never erased from their hearts. "We will not sing the songs of the Lord in a strange land," said the exiles, and the harps, with which they once played and celebrated, remained silent and unused.

God, however, had not forgotten his promises. In the desolation of exile, he sent his prophets to announce, "I will gather you from every place where you are scattered, and I will bring you back to your land. I will purify you from all your evil and give you hearts that love. You will be my people and I will be your God."

THE RETURN TO JERUSALEM

When Cyrus, the king of Persia, conquered Babylon,
his empire became enormous. To better govern the conquered
peoples, he decreed that those who had been deported by the
Babylonians could return to their lands if they wished.
The joy of the Jews was immense: they were free again!
They could finally return to Jerusalem, where they would rebuild
the temple! And they said to each other, "The Lord has done great
things for us." After seventy years of slavery in a foreign land, a
column of about fifty thousand people marched toward the land
of David with horses, mules, donkeys, and camels. When they
arrived in Jerusalem, the elders who remembered the city before
its destruction wept sadly, but the young people were full of
enthusiasm. They rebuilt the temple amidst many difficulties, but
when they finally were able to celebrate Passover again, their
hearts overflowed with joy.
Year after year, many other Jews returned to their homeland.
Among those who returned was Nehemiah, who had been a cupbearer of the king of Persia, and who wanted to restore the mighty
walls of Jerusalem to defend it from its enemies. Nehemiah proved
to be a wise governor and reorganized the life of the city, making
laws to help the poorest people.
Ezra, a scribe and a priest, also arrived in Jerusalem. He had
studied and transcribed the sacred texts that others, before
him, had collected during the time of exile. Thanks to him the
people of Israel could reconstruct their history, laws, and
long-forgotten traditions.

ELEAZAR THE WISE

After the return of the people of Israel to the promised land there was a long period of peace and tranquility until Alexander the Great, king of Macedonia, a region of Greece, defeated the emperor of Persia. Alexander soon became the leader of an empire greater than that of the Persians. It went from the Mediterranean Sea to India, and the Jews were among his subjects.

Alexander tried to bring the culture and customs of Greece to the conquered lands. When he died, his successors continued his work. Among them, one of the most stubborn and cruel was the king Antiochus Epiphanes, who decided to impose by force the pagan culture and the gods of the Greek Olympus. He stripped Jerusalem's temple of its sacred furnishings and ordered that the statue of Zeus be brought there.

Antiochus forbade the Jews to gather in prayer, to respect the Sabbath rest, and to follow their other traditions. Some obeyed, but many others chose to die rather than betray God. Among these was Eleazar, an old scribe, who refused to eat pork, as prohibited by the law of Moses.

To some of the Jews who wanted to pretend to eat pork to save their lives, Eleazar said, "If I pretended to eat pork, it would be a bad example for young people. What would they think, seeing that, at my age, for just a little more life, I gave in to the customs of the pagans?" And he added, "Even if I escaped from the punishment of men, I could not escape from the Almighty."

And he courageously faced martyrdom.

THE FESTIVAL OF LIGHTS

In this difficult period, in a small town called Modein, there was a priest named Mattathias with his five sons, known as the "Maccabees" (which means "hammers") because of their determination. One day the king's officials presented themselves to Mattathias, saying, "You are a man who is esteemed by everyone. If you will be the first to obey the king's command to offer sacrifices to the gods, others will follow you, and the king will reward you with gold and many gifts." Mattathias replied, "Even if everyone else submits to the wishes of the king, my children and I will not betray the covenant our fathers have with God."

So he fled to the mountains with his sons and a group of faithful companions, determined to fight to defend his people from the abuses of Antiochus. Mattathias became the head of a revolt, and after his death his place was taken by his son Judas Maccabeus. When the king sent his army to destroy the rebels, Judas did not lose heart. He encouraged his soldiers to trust the Lord, saying, "It is better for us to die in battle than to see the ruin of our people." And he defeated the enemies.

With his faith and determination, Judas Maccabeus reconquered Jerusalem. When the rebels entered the city, they saw the ruined temple, its burned doors, and the grass growing in its courtyards. Then they purified the sacred space and rebuilt the altar of sacrifices. They burned the incense and lit the lamps of the big lampstand with the oil from a small jar found in the ruins of the temple. The celebrations continued for eight days, but the oil never ran out and the lights kept burning. These were moments of great joy.

To commemorate the re-dedication of the temple, Judas wanted to celebrate a festival every year during the winter for eight days. This is the festival of Hanukkah, also called the Festival of Lights.

THE FAITHFUL GOD

The fruits that arise from violence do not last long. And so, despite the reconquest of Jerusalem, war continued for many years and the Maccabee brothers, one after another, led the Jewish army against the enemies. After the death of Simon, the last of the brothers, their descendants ruled Judea. But power made them jealous of each other and they began to fight for command.
It was in this situation that the empire of Rome conquered Jerusalem and made Herod the Great, a foreigner, the king.

But God had not abandoned his people. He stayed with them step-by-step and was silently preparing a great surprise. People known for their wisdom prepared the people to welcome it, teaching the way of God and the art of living in the right way. One of these was Ben Sirach, a grandfather like many who taught his nephew the law of God and his way of working in history. Ben Sirach wrote, "Consider past generations and ask yourself: Has anyone trusted in the Lord and been disappointed? Or has anyone persevered in fear of the Lord and been abandoned? Or has anyone called upon the Lord and been ignored? Because the Lord is compassionate and merciful."

Ben Sirach was right. Soon the whole world would contemplate the great sign of God's mercy.

NEW TESTAMENT

ZECHARIAH AND ELIZABETH

When Herod was king of Judea, there was an old priest named Zechariah. He and his wife Elizabeth had no children and no longer hoped to have any.

One day, while Zechariah was praying in the temple of Jerusalem, an angel appeared to him in the clouds of incense and said, "The Lord has fulfilled your desire. Elizabeth will have a son, and you will call him John. He will be a great prophet and will prepare the hearts of people for the arrival of the Savior."

Zechariah was surprised and said, "This is impossible. My wife and I are old now."

The angel replied, "I am Gabriel, and I stand in the presence of the Lord. And since you did not believe me, you will remain silent until the birth of the child."

When Zechariah left the temple, he could no longer speak and expressed himself in gestures. Everyone understood that something extraordinary must have happened to him. He returned home and soon his wife Elizabeth realized she was expecting a baby.

MARY RECEIVES NEWS

Six months after these events, the angel Gabriel was sent by God to the town of Nazareth in Galilee. Here lived a young woman named Mary, engaged to Joseph, a carpenter and a descendant of King David.

Mary was alone in her little house. When the angel came in, he greeted her saying, "Rejoice, Mary, the Lord has filled you with his grace." Mary was confused and did not understand. The angel continued, "I announce to you news of great joy. You will soon have a child, and you will call him Jesus. He will reign on the throne of David and his kingdom will have no end."

Mary asked, "How can I have a child? I'm not married yet." And the angel answered, "The Holy Spirit will come upon you and the Lord will overshadow you. The child who will be born will be holy and will be called Son of God. Even Elizabeth, your relative, who all believed to be sterile, expects a child. Nothing is impossible to God."

Then Mary said, "I am the servant of the Lord. Let it be as you said."

And the angel went away.

AN UNEXPECTED VISIT

Mary thought of what had happened to her. She was still full of questions, but at the same time she felt a great sweetness in her heart. She was expecting a child! And Elizabeth was pregnant too! She wanted to share her secret with her. She left in great haste, walking along the long road that led to her village. When Elizabeth saw her coming, she rushed to embrace Mary, and inspired by the Holy Spirit, she told her, "You are blessed among all women, and blessed is the child you carry! The baby in my womb recognized your voice and jumped with joy."

Mary answered, "My heart is bursting with happiness. I'm just a girl, but the Lord has done great things for me! Everyone will call me blessed. The Lord has remembered the promise He made to our fathers, and He has chosen me to help make it happen." Mary stayed with her cousin for three months. Then Elizabeth's son was born. He was called John, and his father Zechariah began to speak again, just as the angel had said.

MARY AND JOSEPH'S MARRIAGE

Mary returned to Nazareth. She could no longer hide that she was having a baby and tried to explain to Joseph what had happened. He was a good man and he loved Mary very much, but he could not understand. He only knew he was not the child's father. The law in these cases required that he break the engagement, but he could not decide.

One night the angel Gabriel spoke to him in a dream, saying, "Joseph, do not be afraid to take Mary as your bride. The child she is expecting is the work of the Holy Spirit. You will call him Jesus and he will be the Savior of his people."

Joseph woke up reassured; he understood what he
had to do. He set his wedding day and, at the end of
the festivities, took Mary with him and brought her to
live in his house.
Meanwhile the days passed, and the birth of Jesus
became ever closer.

JESUS IS BORN IN BETHLEHEM

At that time, the emperor Caesar Augustus ordered the census of all
the populations that were under the dominion of Rome. Everyone
had to be registered in the city where their family came from.
Joseph took Mary with him and set off for Bethlehem of Judea,
the city of David, the shepherd king, his ancestor.
When they reached Bethlehem, Mary realized that she was about to
have her baby. Joseph hurried to find a quiet and secluded lodging,
but houses and inns were full of people who were there for the
census. By now it was night. Finally, they found a place in a stable.
Joseph helped Mary stretch out on the straw and waited. The child
was born.
They called him Jesus, as the angel had said. His mother washed
him, wrapped him in a clean cloth, and put him to sleep in the
manger. Not far away, in the hills, some shepherds spent the night
warming themselves around a fire and guarding their flock.
Suddenly they saw a great light and an angel appeared.
"Do not be afraid," said the angel. "I announce to you a great joy.
In the city of David the Savior was born, who is Christ the Lord.
Go, you will find a child wrapped in a cloth and lying in a manger."
The light increased in intensity and a choir of angels sang,
"Glory to God in the highest heavens and peace on earth to the
people he loves!"
The vision disappeared and immediately the shepherds set off for
Bethlehem. They found Mary, Joseph, and the child in the manger as
the angel had said. They returned happily to their flock praising the
Lord and telling everyone what they had seen and heard.

SIMEON AND ANNA

After forty days, Mary and Joseph went to Jerusalem with the child to present him to the Lord, as was the tradition for first-born children. They brought with them a small offering, a pair of turtledoves, which was the offering of the poor.

When they were in the temple, a very old man approached them. It was Simeon, a righteous and devout man to whom the Holy Spirit had revealed that he would not die without having seen the Savior of Israel. Full of emotion, he took Jesus in his arms and blessed him saying, "Now I can die in peace, because my eyes have seen you."

In the temple lived also a prophetess named Anna. She was eighty-four years old and prayed to the Lord day and night. She too awaited the coming of the Savior, and when she saw the child in Simeon's arms, she recognized him and praised God.

Mary and Joseph were amazed at everything that was happening to them.

THE WISE MEN AND THE STAR

In the meantime, some wise men from the East came to Jerusalem.
They saw a new star appear in the sky and set off to follow it. That
mysterious star, said the ancient prophecies, announced the birth of
a great king.

But near the holy city the star had disappeared, and the wise men
kept asking everyone, "Where is the king of the Jews who was born?
We came to worship him."

At that time, Herod was king of Judea. He was an evil and suspicious
man. He questioned the scribes and the priests about who this new
king was. They said to him, "It is written that the king who will lead
Israel will be born in Bethlehem of Judea."

Herod was cunning, and he summoned the wise men to the palace
and said to them, "Go to Bethlehem. The child you are looking for

is there. Let me know when you find him, so that I too may come to adore him." But he meant something quite different. As soon as the wise men left Jerusalem, the star appeared again in the night sky and led them on the way. They followed it until it stopped over a house in Bethlehem. The wise men were amazed by how poor it was, but when they saw the child in Mary's arms their hearts were filled with joy. They knelt and worshiped him. They offered as gifts the products of their countries: gold, incense, and myrrh. Then, warned by an angel in a dream, they did not go back to Herod and returned to the East by another route.

THE ESCAPE TO EGYPT

Herod was waiting in his palace. He was impatient for news, and when he realized that the wise men had fooled him, he was furious. Who could this new king who threatened his throne be? He had to get rid of him at all costs.

And so he ordered all the male children of Bethlehem under two years old to be killed.

But an angel warned Joseph in a dream, "Get up and take Mary and the baby with you. Flee to Egypt and stay there until I warn you. Herod seeks Jesus to kill him."

Joseph woke up with a start, quickly picked up his few things, helped Mary onto their donkey, put the child in her arms, and fled in the night. When the soldiers of Herod came to Bethlehem, they were long gone. The soldiers went from house to house and killed the children they found. Bethlehem rang with shouts and crying, and the memory of that massacre lasted forever. When King Herod died, the angel appeared to Joseph again in a dream and said, "The danger is over. Take Mary and the child with you and return to the land of Israel." Joseph obeyed, but he decided not to return to Bethlehem, because Herod's son Archelaus, who was as cruel as his father, reigned there now. Instead, he returned with Mary and Jesus to Nazareth of Galilee, the city where they first met.

JESUS AT THE TEMPLE

Years went by quietly in Nazareth. Jesus grew up studying the Scriptures
and learning Joseph's craft. The grace of the Lord was on him.
Every year Mary and Joseph, according to tradition, went to
Jerusalem to celebrate Passover, the feast that recalled the
liberation of the Jews from their slavery in Egypt. It was a journey
of a few days and when he was twelve, Jesus went with his parents.
After the days of the feast, Mary and Joseph joined the pilgrim
caravan to return home. They had lost sight of their son, but they
did not worry about it. "He's with us, among the group of boys,"
they thought. At the end of the day the caravan stopped, the

families gathered to spend the night, and only then did they realize that Jesus had disappeared.

Scared, they retraced their steps. They looked for their son for three days and finally found him in the temple. He was there, sitting among the doctors of the law, listening to them and answering their questions. Then Mary came forward and said to him, "Why did you do that? Your father and I were scared and worried and have looked for you everywhere." Jesus answered, "Why were you looking for me? Do you not know that I must take care of the things of God, my father?" They all returned to Nazareth. Mary did not understand everything, but often thought about what had happened and kept it in her heart.

THE BAPTISM OF JESUS

Jesus was thirty years old. The emperor Tiberius reigned over
the territories of the Roman empire, and Pontius Pilate was the
governor of Judea. At that time, John, the son of Elizabeth and
Zechariah, began to preach on the banks of the Jordan River.
John wore a garment of camel hair, like the ancient prophets, and
ate grasshoppers and wild honey. People came from everywhere to
hear him, and he told them, "Repent of your sins. Change your life,
because the kingdom of heaven is near." Then he baptized them by
immersing them in the waters of the river as a sign of purification.
Many asked him, "Are you the one to come, the Messiah, the one
who will make Israel free?" And John answered, "I baptize you with
water, but the one who comes after me is stronger than me. He will
baptize you with the fire of the Holy Spirit."
When news of these events came to Nazareth, Jesus understood
that the time had come to start his mission.
He left his home and went to the Jordan to be baptized.
As soon as John saw him, he immediately recognized him
and said, "You come to me? It is I who must be baptized
by you!"
But Jesus answered, "It is right this way." He entered
the river and was baptized by John. Suddenly the sky
opened, and the Spirit of God came down on him in the
form of a dove. There was a voice that said, "You are
my son, my beloved one. I will work through you."

JESUS MEETS THE DEVIL IN THE DESERT

After his baptism, Jesus, driven by the Holy Spirit, went to the desert to pray. For forty days and forty nights he did not eat, supported only by the power of the Holy Spirit, but at the end of those days he was hungry.

The devil, seeing him weak, came to tempt him. He said, "If you really are the son of God, turn these stones into bread." But Jesus answered, "Bread is not enough to satisfy hunger. One needs the word that comes from God."

Then the devil brought him to Jerusalem, on the highest point of the temple, and said, "If you really are the son of God, show it!

Jump down and the angels of your Father will come to save you."
But Jesus answered, "It is not right to challenge the Lord by
demanding a miracle."
The devil did not give up. He took Jesus to the top of a very high
mountain and showed him the kingdoms of the earth and said, "I
will give you all the power and glory you desire, if you kneel before
me and worship me." Then Jesus cried out, "Go away, Satan! It is
written, 'You shall love the Lord your God
and you will worship him alone.'"
The devil disappeared and
immediately the angels came
to Jesus and served him.

JESUS CHOOSES TWELVE FRIENDS

Jesus began his preaching in Galilee. He traveled the small towns and fishing villages along the shores of Lake Tiberias, announcing, "This is a blessed time. The kingdom of God is near. Repent and believe in the good news." His words touched the heart and people listened to him in amazement, pressing around him every time he taught.

One day Jesus saw two fishing boats on the beach and the fishermen washing their nets. He climbed into the boat of Simon, called Peter, and asked him to take the boat a little offshore. From there all the people could see him and listen to him easily.

When he had finished teaching, he said to Peter, "Take your boat into the deep water and cast out the nets."

Peter replied, "Teacher, my brother Andrew and I fished all night without catching anything. But if you say so, we'll try again."

They cast their nets and caught so many fish they could not hoist them on the boat. "Help!" they shouted. James and John, who had watched the scene from the beach, came with their boat. There were so many fish in the nets that the two boats almost sank. While the fishermen looked at Jesus full of amazement, Peter threw himself at his feet saying, "Lord, turn away from me, I am a sinner!" Jesus answered, "Do not be afraid, Peter. Follow me, and I will make you fish for people." And they left everything behind and went with him.

Philip, a young man from Bethsaida, the same city where Peter and Andrew lived, also became a disciple of Jesus.

Filled with enthusiasm, he looked for his friend Nathanael, also known as Bartholomew, and found him sitting under a fig tree. He told Nathanael, "I met the one Moses and the prophets spoke about. It is Jesus of Nazareth, the son of Joseph!"

Nathanael looked at him, perplexed. "Imagine that! Has anything good ever come from Nazareth?" he asked.

"Come and see," answered Philip. When Jesus saw Nathanael coming toward him, he said, "Behold an Israelite in whom there is no lie."

"Do you know me?" he asked.

"Before Philip called you, I saw you under the fig tree," answered Jesus. Nathanael gasped. "Teacher, you are truly the king of Israel!"

Jesus, smiling, replied, "Is that all it takes for you to believe in me?

Simon

Judas

James

Thaddaeus

Thomas

Matthew

You'll see things bigger than that. Follow me."

While he was preaching along the shores of the lake, Jesus saw Matthew the tax collector sitting at his workbench. Everyone hated him because he worked for the Roman invaders, and nobody wanted to be his friend. Jesus came up and, feeling sorry for him, said to him, "Follow me." Matthew also got up and followed him.

Many others followed Jesus and became his disciples. From among these Jesus chose twelve friends, whom he called "apostles," who would always be with him. These are their names: Simon Peter and his brother Andrew; James and John, Zebedee's sons; Philip and Bartholomew; Thomas and Matthew; James, son of Alphaeus, and Thaddaeus; Simon the Cananaean and Judas Iscariot.

Bartholomew

hilip

James

John

Andrew

Peter

THE WEDDING AT CANA

There was a wedding feast at Cana in Galilee, a village a few miles from Nazareth. Mary, the mother of Jesus, had been invited and even Jesus arrived at the party accompanied by some of his disciples. The families of the spouses did not have much money and so there was not as much food and drink for the banquet as they needed. Soon the wine began to run low. It was an embarrassing situation and the young couple's wedding party was in danger of ending early. Mary noticed and worried. She said to her son, "They have no more wine." But Jesus did not seem to listen to her.

Mary was not discouraged at all and said to the servants, "Do whatever he tells you." Then Jesus ordered them to fill with water six large stone jars that stood there. As soon as they were filled to the brim, Jesus said, "Now bring a cup to the table master."
The servants were amazed to see that the water had turned into wine. The master of the table, who had not noticed anything, tasted the wine and exclaimed, "It's wonderful! Serve it to the guests."
Then he went to the groom and said, "Everyone serves good wine at the beginning and when the guests have already drunk a lot, they bring the lower quality wine to the table. But you have kept the best wine until now."
The party lasted a long time and the guests were full of joy.

THE BEATITUDES

One morning, seeing that a large crowd had come to hear him,
Jesus climbed to the top of a hill and sat down. People sat around
him on the grass and waited. Jesus began to speak and said,
"Blessed are you who are poor, for the kingdom of heaven will be
yours. Blessed are you who are hungry, for you will be satisfied.
Blessed are you who cry, because you will laugh. Blessed are you
when they hate you and despise you because you are my friends.
On that day, be happy, for your reward is great in heaven."
Everyone listened in silence.
Jesus continued, "Love your enemies and pray for them. It is
easy to love those who love us, but what merit is there in that?

When someone asks for your time, your love, your things, give everything generously without asking for anything in return. Be sons and daughters of your Father in heaven, who is good to all and makes the sun shine on the just and on the unjust."

Jesus said again, "When you pray, do not waste so many words, because your heavenly Father knows what you need even before you ask. Pray with your heart, because the Lord knows your most hidden sorrows and joys. Pray like this:

"Our Father in heaven,
hallowed be your name.
Your kingdom come,
your will be done,
on earth as it is in heaven.
Give us this day our daily bread,
and forgive us our debts
as we forgive our debtors.
Do not let us be tempted,
but deliver us from evil."

JESUS HEALS THE SICK

Among those who came to listen to Jesus every day, there were many
sick people: some who were paralyzed and carried on stretchers, some
who were blind or epileptic or deaf, and even some with unclean
spirits. They came from the farthest places, accompanied by relatives
or supported by friends. Jesus had compassion for their sufferings
and, to show that the kingdom of God was already present, he
healed the sick and freed the ones with unclean spirits.

One day a man covered with leprosy threw himself at Jesus' feet
saying, "Lord, if you want you can heal me." Leprosy was an awful
disease. There was no cure, and those who had it were forced to live
far from everyone else, for fear that they would infect others. And
so those who had the disease suffered both from its pain and from
loneliness and the contempt of other people.

But Jesus was not afraid. He stretched out his hand and, touching
the leper, said, "Be healed!" Immediately the leprosy disappeared.

The news of the miracle spread rapidly, and more and more crowds flocked to Jesus to listen and be healed.

Jesus and his disciples often returned to Capernaum, the village on the lake of Tiberias, where his first friends had welcomed him. While he was there, Jesus entered a synagogue one day on the Sabbath and began to teach. Many came to listen to him, and among them there was a man with a paralyzed hand. The Pharisees thought, "What will Jesus do? It is Saturday, which is the Sabbath, and no one is allowed to perform any activity, including healing, on the Sabbath." Jesus, knowing their thoughts, said to the man with a paralyzed hand, "Get up and come here." Then he continued, addressing the Pharisees, "What is it better to do on the Sabbath? Good or evil? To save people or abandon them?" But the Pharisees were silent. Saddened by the hardness of their hearts, Jesus said to the man, "Stretch out your hand!" The man did, and it was completely healed.

On another day, still in Capernaum, people gathered to see Jesus and listen to him. Four men arrived carrying a paralyzed friend lying on a stretcher. They wanted Jesus to heal him, but it was impossible to get close to him; the house where he sat was packed and the crowd stood at the door and in the streets all around. But the four were not discouraged. They carried the paralyzed man up onto the roof of the house, moved the boards and the branches that covered it, and using ropes lowered him on his stretcher into the middle of the room, right in front of Jesus.

Touched by their faith, Jesus said, "Son, your sins are forgiven." There were some scribes and Pharisees there who began to mumble among themselves, "What is he saying? Only God can forgive our sins!"

Jesus knew what they were thinking and asked, "What is easier? To say, 'Your sins are forgiven' or 'Get up and walk'? To show you that God has given me the power to forgive sins here on earth I say to you, get up and walk!"

The paralyzed man got up, took his stretcher, and, to the amazement of everyone, walked happily on his feet.

THE STORM ON THE LAKE

It was evening and Jesus, after having preached for the whole day on the shore of the lake, said to his disciples, "Let's go to the other shore." They took the boat and left. The boat sailed across the water and Jesus was so tired that he laid down on a mat and fell asleep. While they were offshore, the weather suddenly changed and a violent storm broke out. The wind shook the boat and the waves

were almost sinking it. But Jesus continued to sleep. The disciples, frightened, woke him up and said, "Teacher, we are going to sink! Do you not care about our lives?"

Then Jesus stood up, threatened the wind, and said to the lake, "Peace! Be still!" The wind stopped abruptly and the waters returned calm. Then he turned to his disciples and said, "Why are you afraid? You are with me! Have you still no faith?" The disciples looked at him full of wonder and fear and said to each other, "Who is this man? Even the wind and the waves obey him!"

FIVE LOAVES OF BREAD AND TWO FISH

Jesus' life was intense. People did not leave him in peace. Everyone wanted to listen to him, ask him for advice, and bring sick people to him. One day, when he reached the lake, he found the crowd waiting for him. When he saw them, Jesus felt great love; they were like scattered sheep, without a shepherd to take care of them. Then he forgot he was tired and decided to stay with them. He consoled the sad and healed the sick. To everyone he spoke of the kingdom of God. Meanwhile, the hours passed, the sun was setting, and nobody had eaten since the morning. The disciples were worried and said to Jesus, "It's already late. Send them away so they can go to the

villages around here to look for something to eat."
Jesus answered, "They do not have to go away. You give them
something to eat." They looked at him in astonishment, and Philip
said, "Where do we find bread for all these people? We are in an
isolated place. And anyway, two hundred denarii would not even
be enough to buy a piece of bread for each one!" Andrew, Peter's
brother, said, "There's a boy here who has five loaves and two fish.
But it's so little!" Then Jesus said, "Have them sit down." They
all sat on the grass, about five thousand people. Jesus took the
five loaves and the two fish. He looked up to heaven and blessed
and broke them. Then he invited his disciples to pass it out to the
crowd. And the more they distributed, the more the loaves and the
fish multiplied. Everyone ate their fill. And when they had finished,
the disciples gathered twelve baskets of broken pieces.

JESUS IS TRANSFIGURED

After dismissing the crowd, while they were near the villages in the district of Caesarea Philippi, Jesus asked his disciples, "Who do people say that I am?" And they said, "Some say you are a great prophet, others say you are the prophet Elijah who has arisen again among us, others Jeremiah, others John the Baptist."

Jesus asked them, "But who do you say that I am?" The disciples were silent. They looked at each other without finding the courage to respond. Then Peter spoke and said, "You are the Christ, the son of the living God!"

Jesus said, "Blessed are you, Peter! What you say you did not understand by yourself, but it was revealed to you by my Father in heaven. And you will be the rock on which I will build my Church, and the powers of evil will not be able to destroy it." He then ordered his disciples not to tell anyone that he was the Savior. From that moment Jesus began to explain to his disciples that he would have to suffer a lot, be killed, and rise from the dead on the third day. But his disciples could not understand what he meant.

A few days later, Jesus took Peter, James, and John with him and went up a mountain to pray. As he prayed, the disciples saw his face shine like the sun and his robe became white and shining. Next to Jesus appeared Moses and the prophet Elijah and they spoke with him.

The disciples thought they were dreaming, and Peter said, "Lord, it is good for us to be here. We will build three tents here, one for you, one for Moses, and one for Elijah." But as soon as he had finished speaking, a bright cloud enveloped them and they heard a voice saying, "This is my beloved son. Listen to him!" Then they fell prostrate with their faces on the ground, full of fear and fright. When they raised their eyes, Elijah and Moses had disappeared and Jesus was there alone. As they descended from the mountain, Jesus told them not to tell anyone what had happened until his resurrection.

THE SAD MOTHER AND FATHER

Along the journey, Jesus passed by Nain, a small town near
Nazareth. Arriving at the gates of the city, a crowd of people came
to meet him. It was the funeral of a boy, the only son of a woman
left widowed. When Jesus saw her cry in despair, he was moved,
approached her and said, "Woman, do not cry." Then he signaled to
the coffin bearers to stop and said, "Young man, I say to you, rise!"
The dead boy sat up. Jesus took the young man's hand and placed
it in his mother's hand. The woman was now crying tears of
joy. Everyone was stunned, and some said, "A great prophet has
risen among us!" And others said, "God has visited his people."
Something similar happened in Capernaum, too. A man named
Jairus, one of the leaders of the synagogue, came to Jesus one day
and threw himself at his feet saying, "My little daughter is dying!
Come with me, save her!"

Jesus was moved and followed him, but the crowd held him back and slowed him down. Along the way, a servant of Jairus reached them and said to his master, "It's too late, your daughter is dead. It is no longer necessary to disturb the teacher."

But Jesus intervened, saying, "Do not be afraid. Keep trusting in me!" And they continued on their way home. When they arrived, they found people crying and wailing. "Why do you make so much noise?" Jesus said. "The child is not dead. She's only sleeping." They thought he was crazy. Then he drove them all out of the room where the child was and let only the parents and his disciples stay. He sat down next to the girl and took her hand, saying, "Little girl, get up!"

The girl stood up and smiled, as if after a long sleep. "Now she's fine. She will be hungry, give her food to eat," Jesus said.

THE FARMER

It was nice to listen to Jesus; people never got tired of him.
Nobody had ever talked to them like that. His words touched the
heart. Even difficult ideas, when he offered them, became simple.
He often told stories, called parables, which took examples from
everyday life.

One day Jesus said, "Listen. A farmer went to the field to plant
seeds. Some seeds fell on the path, and immediately the birds came
and ate them up. Other seeds fell among the stones, where there
was little soil, and as soon as the shoots sprouted the sun scorched
them and they died. Other seeds fell among thorns, and when the
thorns grew up they choked the shoots. Part of the seeds fell on
good soil, and when they sprouted they gave much fruit."

Jesus then explained the parable: "The farmer is God who never
tires of announcing his kingdom to people. The seed is the word of
God and the soil is people's hearts. The seed that falls on the road
is like someone who hears the word of God but does not put it into
practice. The seed that falls among the stones is like someone who
welcomes the word of God but becomes discouraged the first time
things get hard. The seed that falls among thorns is like someone
who is distracted by money and daily worries. The seed that falls on
good soil is like someone who accepts the word of God and does it."

THE KINGDOM OF HEAVEN IS LIKE...

Jesus used these stories to explain the kingdom of heaven:
"The kingdom of heaven is like a mustard seed, the smallest of all
the seeds on earth. But once it has grown, it becomes the largest
plant in the garden and birds can nest in its branches.
"The kingdom of heaven is like the yeast that a woman mixed in
with flour. When the dough is all leavened she will cook it and it
will make a lot of bread.
"The kingdom of heaven is like a treasure hidden in a field,
which someone finds by chance. Full of joy, that person hides the
treasure again, then runs to sell everything to buy that field.
"The kingdom of heaven is like a merchant who goes in search
of precious pearls. When he finds the most precious pearl of all,
he sells what he owns and buys it. And he is happy to have that
single pearl."
To those who asked him, "But when will the kingdom of heaven
come?" Jesus answered, "The kingdom of
heaven does not come in a way that
attracts attention. No one will be able
to say, 'Look, here it is' or 'There it is.'
The kingdom of heaven is already among
you."

THE GOOD SAMARITAN

One day, among the crowd listening to Jesus there was a scholar of the law who knew the Scriptures well. To test Jesus he asked him, "What must I do to have eternal life?"

Jesus answered with a question: "What do the Scriptures say?"

"To love God with all my heart and with all my strength and to love my neighbor as myself," replied the scholar of the law.

"Do this and you will live," Jesus said.

But the scholar of the law did not want to give up and asked again, "Who is my neigbor?"

Jesus answered by telling this parable: "A man was traveling from Jerusalem to Jericho, when he was assaulted by bandits. They robbed him of everything and

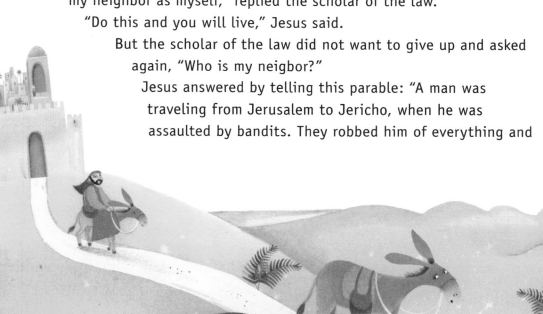

beat him, leaving him half dead on the side of the road. A priest
and then a Levite, a servant in the temple, passed by on that
same road, but neither stopped to help him and quickly turned
away from that dangerous place. A foreigner passed by, a Samaritan,
and when he saw the man in that condition, felt sorry for him.
He stopped, washed his wounds, loaded him on his donkey,
and took him to the nearest inn. The next day, having to leave,
he gave money to the innkeeper saying, 'Take care of him and,
if it is necessary, I will give you more money when I
come back.'"
Jesus ended by asking, "Which of the three was that
poor fellow's neighbor?" The scholar of the law replied,
"The one who helped him." Then Jesus said to him,
"Go and act like the Samaritan."

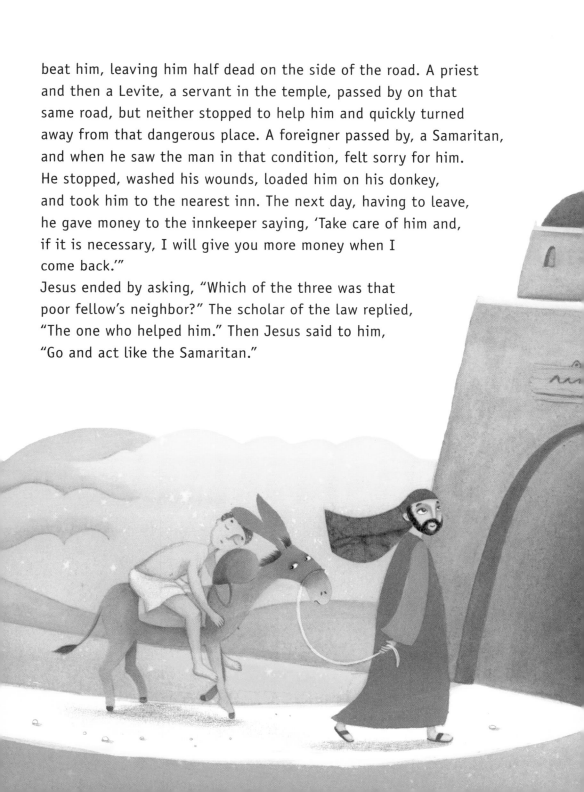

THE LOST SHEEP

Even sinners approached Jesus to listen to him, and he did not refuse his friendship to anyone. The scribes and the Pharisees were scandalized, saying, "It is not right to be friends with those who do evil. Jesus even eats with them."

Then Jesus told this parable: "A man had a hundred sheep. He loved them all and knew them one by one. One day he realized that one of the sheep had disappeared. He left the other ninety-nine and went in search of the lost sheep. He looked for it everywhere until he found it. Full of joy, he put it on his shoulders and when he got home, he called friends and neighbors and said, 'Come, let's have a party because I found my sheep!'"

Jesus said, "There is more joy in heaven for one sinner who repents than for ninety-nine righteous people who need no repentance."

THE TWO SONS

To help people understand how good God is and how ready to forgive, Jesus told this other parable. "A very rich man had two sons. One day the younger son said to his father, 'Give me my share of inheritance. I want to leave this house and get to know the world.' His father was sorry, but he did as his son had asked him. After packing his things, the young man left for a distant country where he spent all his money on parties and fun. Left without a penny, he tried to make a living, but the only one who gave him a job was a farmer, who sent him to feed the pigs.

"A famine had fallen on that country and the young man stood there, alone and hungry, and was even jealous of the pigs, that at least had scraps to eat. Then he began to think, 'What am I doing here? At home, the servants are treated well and have plenty of bread. I'll go back to my father, ask him for forgiveness and propose to work for him as if I were one of his paid workers.' He got up and left. While he was still far away, his father saw him coming. The father's heart began to beat hard with joy. He ran to meet his son and threw his arms around his neck. The son was confused and excited. 'Father, I was wrong. I do not deserve to be called your son,' he said. But the father called the servants and said, 'Hurry! Bring here the most beautiful clothes and put them on him! Get the fatted calf from the stable, kill it and roast it! We are having a party tonight, because the son I thought was lost came home.'"

But the parable was not yet finished. Jesus continued, "The oldest

son was working in the fields. When he came back
in the evening and he found out that the party was
for his brother, he got angry and refused to enter the
house. The father then went out to beg him, but he replied,
'Listen! I have always done my duty. I have never disobeyed
you, and you have never even given me a goat to celebrate
with my friends. Now this good-for-nothing is back after
spending all your money, and you not only forgive him,
but you also throw him a big party!'
"The father answered him, 'Son, you are always with me, and the
things that belong to me are yours. But your brother was dead
and now he has come back to life. He was lost and now has
been found again.'"

THE TALENTS

God is a generous father who fills his children with gifts, but each has a particular task. To explain this, Jesus told a parable that spoke of coins of great value, called talents.

"Before leaving for a long journey, a man called his three servants. To the first servant he gave five talents, to the second two, and to the third one talent, according to the abilities of each. The first two immediately traded with them to make more money. But the third servant, was a fearful and suspicious man. He dug a hole in the ground and hid his talent.

"After a long time the master returned, called the servants, and asked them to show what they did with the talents.

"The first servant said, 'Master, you gave me five talents. Here are

five more.' 'Well done! You have been a faithful servant,' replied the master. 'Come and celebrate with me.' The servant who had received two talents said, 'Look, Master, I have earned two more talents.' 'You too have been a good and faithful servant,' said the master. 'Come and celebrate with me.'

"The third servant spoke last, saying, 'Sir, I did not want to take any risks. I buried the talent you gave me underground where it was safe. Here it is!' 'What?' replied the master. 'You knew I would come back and ask you for my money with interest. You could have invested it and make it profit!' He then ordered that his talent be given to those who had worked harder, and that servant was sent away.

"When the Lord returns to judge the world," Jesus said, "he will ask you about the love he has given you. Do not hide what you have received but multiply it for the good of all."

THE TWO HOUSES

Jesus asked those who gathered to listen to him, "Why do you seek me and call me 'Lord, Lord' and then do not do what I tell you?" One day he told them this parable: "Whoever hears my words and puts them into practice is like a wise man who, determined to build a house, digs its foundations in the rock. Rain comes, rivers flow, and winds blow, but the house is solid and safe because it is built on rock.

"Whoever listens to my words and does not put them into practice is like a foolish man who builds his house on sand. The rain comes, the rivers flow, and the winds blow and his house is ruined because it is built on what cannot support it."

JESUS AND THE CHILDREN

One day, while they were going along the road,
there was a lively discussion among the disciples.
Jesus said nothing, but later he asked, "What
were you talking about today along the road?" The
disciples had discussed who was the greatest among
them, but now they were silent.

Then Jesus made them sit around him, called a child,
and said, "He who wants to be great must make himself
as small as this child. In the eyes of God true greatness
is that of those who are humble and put themselves at the
service of all. Remember: whoever welcomes one of these children
in my name, welcomes me."

Meanwhile, the people took the children to Jesus to bless them. But
the disciples turned them away. Jesus rebuked them, saying, "Let
the children come to me. Do not stop them. The kingdom of heaven
belongs to those who are like them."

Then he hugged the children and
blessed them one by one.

A NIGHTTIME VISIT

There was a Pharisee named Nicodemus. He was a scholar of the law. Some scholars of the law did not like Jesus, but Nicodemus wanted to meet the man everyone was talking about. He waited until night to come to Jesus and said to him, "Teacher, I know that you have the power to work miracles and that you have been sent by God."

Jesus answered him, "No one can see the kingdom of God without being born from above."

Nicodemus was confused and asked, "What does it mean to be 'born from above'? No one can be born more than once."

"We are born when we come to life, but we are also born when we change our way of life, letting ourselves be guided by the Spirit of God. It is this second birth that I am speaking to you about," said Jesus.

Nicodemus again asked, "How can this happen?"

"You are a teacher of Israel, you should know these things," answered Jesus. "Anyone who lives in love every day is a new person and every day is reborn!"

Nicodemus did not understand everything that Jesus told him, but from that moment he loved him and became his friend.

THE WOMAN AT THE WELL

While he was traveling through Samaria, Jesus stopped near a well to rest. A woman with a water jar came to the well to draw water. It was noon and very hot, and Jesus said to the woman, "Give me a drink." "How come you, who are a Jew, ask me, a Samaritan woman, for a drink? There is a bad relationship between our two peoples," the woman observed.

Jesus replied, "If you knew who was asking you for a drink, you would ask him to quench your thirst with living water."

The woman did not understand Jesus' strange words and said, "The well is deep, and you do not even have a bucket to draw it out! Where would you get this living water?"

"Whoever drinks the water from this well will be thirsty again. But whoever drinks my water will never be thirsty," Jesus told her. "Give me this water, then, so I will not need to come here any more," the unhappy woman said. "Call your husband," Jesus told her. "I have no husband," the woman replied. "I know," Jesus went on. "You have had five husbands, and the man you live with now is not your husband." The woman looked at him in amazement. "How do you know? Are you a prophet? So tell me, where should we worship God? My people worship him on this mountain, but your people say that we must worship him in the temple of Jerusalem." Jesus told her, "Neither on this mountain nor in Jerusalem. We worship God with our hearts and with our lives. This is true prayer. Only in this way can we experience the action of the Spirit of God." The woman went on, "I know that the Messiah is coming, and when he comes he will teach us everything."

"I am he, the one who is speaking to you," said Jesus.
The woman dropped her water jar, ran to the city, and began to
exclaim to everyone she met, "Come quickly! There is a man who
told me everything I have ever done! Is he the Messiah?"
The Samaritans from the city came to him and listened to him
speak. Then they said to the woman, "Now we too believe that Jesus
is the Savior of the world." And Jesus stayed with them for two days.

THE MAN IN THE TREE

A man named Zacchaeus lived in the city of Jericho. He had become rich by collecting taxes on behalf of the Romans and taking extra money from the people for himself. People knew about his dishonesty and hated him. One day the rumor spread that Jesus had arrived in the city and everyone rushed into the street. Even Zacchaeus was curious to see the Teacher everyone was talking about. But he was short, and even though he stretched and stood on tiptoe, he could not see over the heads of the people in front of him. So Zacchaeus ran ahead and climbed a tree. "Jesus will pass by here!" he thought. When Jesus passed under the tree, he looked up and said, "Zacchaeus, come down quickly, because today I must stay at your house." Everyone murmured, "Is he really going to go to the home of that dishonest person?"

But Zacchaeus was bursting with joy. Jesus had noticed him! He wanted to be his friend! And when Jesus came to his house, he welcomed him saying, "Lord, I want to give half of my goods to the poor, and if I have stolen from anyone, I will give him back four times as much." Jesus answered: "Zacchaeus, salvation has come to this house today. I came to look for and save those like you who were lost."

BLIND BARTIMAEUS

Coming out of Jericho, Jesus and his disciples met a blind man
named Bartimaeus, a beggar, who was sitting by the roadside.
As soon as the blind man understood that Jesus was passing by,
he began to shout out and say, "Son of David, have mercy on me!"
Someone tried to silence him, but Bartimaeus shouted even louder.
"Son of David, have mercy on me!"
Jesus stopped and said, "Call him here."
They went to him and said, "Come on, get up! Jesus wants to see
you." The blind man was very happy, threw off his cloak, jumped up,
and went to him.
Jesus asked him, "Friend, what do you want me to do for you?"
And the blind man answered, "My Teacher, let me see again."
And Jesus said to him, "Go, your faith has saved you."
At these words, Bartimaeus regained his sight. Filled with joy, he
began to follow Jesus, becoming his disciple.

JESUS CRIES FOR HIS FRIEND

On the way to Jerusalem, there was the village called Bethany, where two sisters and their brother, Martha, Mary, and Lazarus, lived. They were Jesus' friends and always welcomed him in their home. When he visited, Mary often sat at Jesus' feet without thinking of anything else. Martha, on the other hand, kept busy with many chores to show Jesus how much she cared about him.

One day Lazarus became very ill, and the sisters sent a message to the Teacher. Jesus loved Lazarus very much, but strangely he did not hurry to visit his friend. When he finally arrived in Bethany, Lazarus was already dead. Martha ran to meet Jesus and threw herself crying at his feet. She told him, "If you had been here, my brother would not have died!" Jesus told her, "Your brother will rise again."

"I know he will be resurrected at the end of time," replied Martha. And Jesus said, "I am the resurrection and the life. Whoever believes in me does not die but will live forever. Do you believe this?" Martha replied, "Yes, Lord, I believe it."

Martha then went to call her sister Mary, and she too threw herself at Jesus' feet crying. Jesus was sad and cried too. Then he asked to go to the tomb of Lazarus, a cave sealed by a large stone, and he ordered, "Remove the stone." Martha said, "Teacher, our brother has been in the grave for four days. There will be a bad smell!" Jesus answered, "Didn't I tell you that if you believe you will see the glory of God?" They removed the stone. After praying to the Father, Jesus cried with a loud voice, "Lazarus, come out!" And Lazarus walked out of the tomb alive, still wrapped in the burial strips of cloth. Jesus said, "Unbind him and let him go." Many witnessed this miracle, and many believed in him, but others went to the Pharisees and chief priests and told them what Jesus had done. "What can we do?" they asked. "If we do not stop him, everyone will believe in him." And from then on, they decided to find a way to kill Jesus.

THE FORGIVEN SINNER

The Pharisees and the scholars of the law were more and more
worried, because Jesus spent time with Samaritans and sinners.
So they tried in every way to make him look bad, so people
would stop listening to every word he said.
One morning Jesus was preaching in the temple of Jerusalem.
Suddenly there were shouts. A group of Pharisees arrived,
dragging a woman pitilessly. "Teacher," they said, "this woman
has cheated on her husband. According to the law of Moses,
she must be stoned to death. What do you say?" They were
thinking, "Let's see what he does. If he condemns this woman,
we will say that his preaching about forgiveness is just a lie.
If he does not condemn her, we will have proof that he does
not respect the law."
At first, Jesus did not answer. He seemed distracted. But they
insisted, "Tell us what you think."
Then Jesus said, "Whoever has never committed a sin can be the
first to throw a stone at her." He bent down and began to write
with his finger in the dust. Everyone was silent,
then one by one, they left, starting with the elders.
The woman was left alone. Jesus looked up and said,
"Woman, where are your accusers? Has no one condemned you?"
"No one, sir," the woman replied.
Jesus said to her, "Neither do I condemn you. Go,
and from now on do not sin again."

THE COSTLY PERFUME

Before the feast of Passover, Jesus returned with his disciples
to Bethany, where Lazarus, Martha, and Mary welcomed him to
their home. Martha, as usual, prepared dinner for the guests.
Meanwhile, Mary took a vase of precious perfume, knelt, and
poured it on Jesus' feet. Then she wiped them with her hair. The
intense fragrance of the perfume spread throughout the house.
Everyone was surprised. Judas Iscariot, one of the apostles, was
shocked and said, "Why waste such an expensive perfume? Why
not sell it and give the money to the poor?" But he was not
sincere; he did not really care about the poor.
"Leave her alone, Judas. Hers is a gesture of love," Jesus replied.
"You will always have the poor with you, but you will not have me
forever. This perfume was not wasted. She anointed my body to
prepare it for burial."
To those who were listening, these words seemed mysterious, but
they would soon understand.

HOSANNA TO THE SON OF DAVID!

The next day, Jesus walked with his disciples toward Jerusalem.
When they were on the Mount of Olives, now in sight of the city,
Jesus sent two disciples into a nearby village saying, "You will
find a donkey tied with her colt next to her. Untie them and bring
them to me. If someone asks you what you are doing, answer, 'The
Lord needs them.'"

They did as he had ordered. After they brought the two animals,
they stretched their cloaks on the donkey and Jesus sat on it.
A large crowd had gathered in Jerusalem for the feast of Passover.
When word got out that Jesus was coming, people came to meet
him waving palm branches and spreading their cloaks on the road
as he passed. Many had witnessed the miracles he had performed
and now they shouted joyfully, "Hosanna to the Son of David!

Blessed is he who comes in the name of the Lord! Hosanna in the highest heaven!" They accompanied him into the city, acclaiming him as the peace-bearer king announced by the prophets.

The Pharisees and the chief priests were furious, and they wanted to silence the crowd. They said to Jesus, "But do you not hear what they are saying? Reproach them!"

Jesus replied, "If they were silent, the stones would cry out."

The chief priests held a meeting. "Now we have had enough," they said to each other. "We must act quickly. If we do not intervene immediately, they will make him king. Then it will be too late." They did not know what to do. But then Judas Iscariot, one of the twelve apostles, helped them decide. He went secretly to them and said, "What will you give me if I give you Jesus?" And they promised him thirty silver coins. From that moment Judas looked for a chance to get Jesus arrested.

THE WASHING OF THE FEET

On the evening of the Passover supper, Jesus and the apostles gathered in a room. Before he sat down at the table, Jesus took off his cloak, took a towel, and tied it around his waist. Then he poured water into a basin, knelt, and began to wash his friends' feet. The apostles were surprised, and Peter objected, "Lord, will you wash my feet?" Jesus answered him, "You do not understand now, but you will understand later. If I do not wash your feet, you will not be able to fully share what I am and live."

When he had finished this, he sat down at the table and said,

"You call me Lord and Teacher. And you are right, because I am.
If therefore I who am the Lord and the Teacher have washed your
feet, you must also serve one another. I have given you an
example to follow."

After he said these things, Jesus became sad and declared,
"Tonight one of you will betray me."

The apostles were stunned and looked at each other, saying,
"But who is he talking about?"

John, who was seated next to him, asked him, "Lord, who is it?"

Jesus answered, "It is the one to whom I will give a piece of
bread when I have dipped it in the dish."

BREAD AND WINE

While they were eating, Jesus took the bread, said a prayer of blessing, broke it, and gave a piece to each of the apostles, saying, "Take and eat it. This is my body." Then he took a cup of wine, blessed it, and handed it to the apostles, saying, "Drink it, all of you. This is my blood, shed for the new covenant between God and humanity for the forgiveness of sins. Do this in memory of me."
Judas took his piece of bread, got up, and went out into the night.

Knowing that he had to die, that night Jesus talked with his friends for a long time to prepare them for what would happen. "Do not be frightened. I'm going to prepare a place for you, and one day we'll be together again." And he added, "If you do what I command you, you will remain forever in my love. This is my commandment: love one another as I have loved you. No one has a greater love than this: to give their lives for their friends. And you are my friends. I tell you these things because I want you to have peace and joy." And he concluded by saying, "In the world you will go through many trials and suffering but have courage. I have conquered the world!"

THE GARDEN OF GETHSEMANE

After having sung the Passover hymn together, they went out and headed for the Mount of Olives. As they walked, Jesus said, "You all will deny you know me and leave me alone."

"Even if everyone else does that, I will not!" Peter insisted. "Even if it costs me my own life, I will not deny you!"

But Jesus answered him, "Peter, tonight, before the cock crows, you will deny me three times."

They reached a place called Gethsemane and Jesus said to the apostles, "Sit here while I pray." Then, feeling sadness overcome him, he asked Peter, John, and James to follow him. "Stay awake with me, for I am sad and I need to have you close." He went away a little from them and prostrated himself with his face on the ground, praying, "Father, please, keep me from this suffering. But not my will, but yours be done."

Then he went to his friends and found them asleep. He shook Peter: "You're asleep? Can you not stay awake just one hour with me? You too should pray. Be ready." He went away again to pray to the Father and, when he returned, he found them asleep again.

He left them again and when he returned for the third time he said, "Go on sleeping. My hour has arrived. Here comes the one who will betray me."

As he was saying these things, a group of armed men approached carrying torches. Judas was with them and told them, "The one I will kiss is him. Arrest him!" He approached Jesus and said, "Hello, Teacher," and kissed him. Jesus answered, "Friend, with a kiss you betray me?" Immediately the others came forward and took Jesus. Peter's reaction was violent. He seized a sword and hit a servant of

the high priest, cutting his ear off. But Jesus said, "That's enough!"
He touched the servant's wound and healed it. Then he let himself
be taken away. Then the disciples abandoned him and fled.

PETER'S DENIAL

They led Jesus to the house of Caiaphas, the high
priest, where the chief priests, the scribes, and the
elders were gathered. Peter had followed him from afar,
into the courtyard of the palace, and now he was sitting by
the fire among the servants, watching what was happening.
The chief priests sought an excuse to condemn him to death and
questioned many false witnesses, but they could not find any fault
to accuse him of. Jesus was silent and did not answer any of his
accusers' questions. Caiphas finally stood up and asked, "Are you
the Christ, the son of God?" Jesus answered, "Yes, I am."
Then Caiaphas cried out, "Did you hear, everyone? He blasphemed.
What need do we still have of witnesses?"
They all shouted, "Put him to death! Put him to death!" And they
spit on him and beat him.
Meanwhile, a young servant approached Peter and, after looking
at him carefully, said, "I have already seen you. You were with
the Nazarene!" Peter denied it, saying, "I don't know what you're
talking about!" But the man insisted and told the others that were
there, "I recognize him! He's one of them."
Peter denied it again, saying, "I tell you that you're wrong!"
But one of the other servants spoke up and said, "It's true. You
are one of them, too. You have the same accent."
Then Peter, frightened, said, "No! I swear! I do not know that man."
At that moment the cock crowed. Peter remembered the words of
Jesus: "Before the cock crows, you will deny me three times."
And he burst into tears.

JESUS IS BROUGHT TO PILATE

At the first light of dawn, Jesus was delivered to Pontius Pilate, the Roman governor of Judea, because no death sentence could be carried out without his consent.

Judas Iscariot was in the middle of the crowd and seeing Jesus pass he was overcome with remorse. He returned to the chief priests and said, "I have betrayed an innocent man. Take your money back!" But they said, "We do not care. Do what you want with it." Then Judas threw away the thirty coins. He could no longer bear to live and went to hang himself.

Meanwhile Pilate questioned Jesus, "Are you the king of the Jews?" Jesus answered, "You say so."

"They accuse you of many things. What do you have to say in your defense?" But Jesus was silent. Pilate knew that Jesus had been brought to him because of envy and sought a way to free him.

It was the custom that during Passover a condemned man chosen by the people was freed. In the prison there was a rebel named Barabbas. Pilate turned to the crowd outside the palace of the praetorium and said, "Whom do you want me to release: Jesus or Barabbas?"

Urged by the chief priests, the people cried out, "Barabbas!"

Pilate said again: "What do you want me to do with the one you call the king of the Jews?" "Crucify him!" they answered. Pilate asked, "What did he do wrong?" "Crucify him!" they repeated angrily.

The crowd was becoming more and more upset, and Pilate, seeing that he could not change their minds, had water brought and washed his hands in front of them all saying, "I will do as you ask. But know that I am not responsible for the death of this man." Barabbas was freed, and Jesus was given to the Roman soldiers, who stripped him and whipped him until he bled.

When they had finished, they threw a red cloak over his shoulders, put a crown of brambles and thorns on his head, and in his hands they put a staff like a scepter. Kneeling in front of him they said, "Hail, king of the Jews!" Then they tore off his coat and put his clothes back on. And putting a heavy cross on his shoulders, they set out for the place of execution.

THE CRUCIFIXION

During his walk to Golgotha, a large crowd that included many women followed Jesus, crying. Several times Jesus collapsed on the ground under the weight of the cross, so the guards, in order not to waste time, stopped a man, a certain Simon of Cyrene, and forced him to carry the cross in his place.

When they came to the place of execution, Jesus was nailed to the cross and with him two thieves. As the crosses were raised, Jesus said, "Father, forgive them. They do not know what they are doing." The soldiers and chief priests mocked him, saying, "Let's see if you can save yourself now, king of the Jews!"

Even one of the thieves insulted him, saying, "See what they've done to you! Did not you say you were the Savior? Then save yourself and save us."

The thief on the other side, reproached him. "Soon you are going to die, and you still act like that? We have been condemned for our faults, but he is innocent." Then, turning to Jesus, he said, "When you are in your kingdom, remember me."

Jesus answered, "Today you will be with me in heaven."

At the foot of the cross stood Mary, his mother, with a group of women who were comforting her and the youngest of the apostles, John. Jesus turned to Mary and said, "Woman, here is your son." And to John, "Here is your mother." From then on, John took Mary to live with him.

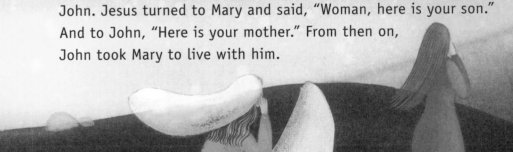

JESUS DIES ON THE CROSS

The hours passed slowly and Jesus on the cross suffered greatly.
From midday, dark clouds covered the sun and there was a great
darkness. At about three o'clock in the afternoon, Jesus cried out,
"My God, my God, why have you forsaken me?" A soldier rushed to
give him a drink, extending a sponge soaked in vinegar with a stick.
Jesus said again, "Father, into your hands I deliver my spirit."
Then he lowered his head to his chest and died.
At that moment, the earth shook, and the veil of the temple was
torn in half. The centurion, seeing how Jesus died, exclaimed,
"Truly this man was the Son of God!"

Evening came. It was the eve of Saturday, the Sabbath day.
Joseph of Arimathea, a disciple, courageously presented himself
to Pilate and asked for the body of Jesus, to bury him. Pilate
granted it to him. Then, helped by Nicodemus, the one who had
gone to Jesus at night, they lowered his body from the cross,
wrapped it in linen cloths, and laid it in a tomb carved into rock.
Then they rolled a large stone in front of the entrance. The women
who had followed Jesus under the cross stood watching.

THE EMPTY TOMB

The day after the Sabbath, early in the morning, the women went to visit the tomb with aromatic oils to embalm Jesus' body. They found the stone removed and the tomb empty. Shocked, they immediately rushed to tell the disciples, but only Peter and John listened to them and rushed to the tomb. When they entered, they saw the burial cloths that had wrapped Jesus' limbs, as if his body had disappeared; there was no trace of him. And filled with amazement, they returned home. Meanwhile Mary of Magdala, a woman whom Jesus had freed from great suffering, stood at the entrance to the tomb and cried. While tears rolled down her cheeks, she saw two angels dressed in

white sitting where the body had been laid. "Woman, why are you crying?" they asked her. "They have taken my Lord away and I do not know where he is!" she answered and, turning her head, she saw Jesus standing before her, but she did not recognize him.

"Woman, why are you crying? Who are you looking for?" asked Jesus. Mary thought it was the gardener and said, "If you have carried him away, I beg you, tell me where you have laid him."

Then Jesus called her by name: "Mary!"

She fell to her knees and held out her hands to him, saying, "Teacher!"

But Jesus said to her, "Do not hold me back, I have not yet ascended to the Father. Go to my brothers and tell them, 'I am going to my Father and your Father, my God and your God.'" Mary of Magdala ran to the disciples and announced, "I have seen the Lord!"

THE ROAD TO EMMAUS

Following these events, two disciples decided to return to their home
in Emmaus, a village not far from Jerusalem. While they were talking
to each other, very worked up, a traveler came up and walked with
them. It was Jesus, but they did not recognize him. He listened to
them for a while and then asked, "What are you talking about?"
They looked at him sadly. One of the two, named Cleopas, said, "You
must be the only one who does not know what has happened in
these days. They are not talking about anything else in Jerusalem!"
Then he continued, "We were talking about Jesus of Nazareth,
a great prophet. The chief priests and the Roman authorities
condemned him to death and crucified him. We had hoped he was
the liberator of Israel. This morning some women have astounded
us, claiming to have seen him alive. Our friends went to the grave,
but they found it empty and the body disappeared." The stranger
said, "How foolish you are! Do you not understand that the Messiah
had to go through these trials to accomplish his mission?" And he

began to explain all the things in the Scriptures that were about him. The two listened to him attentively and, as the traveler spoke, their bitterness and disappointment turned into a sense of peace. When they were close to the village, the traveler walked ahead as if he were going on. But they still wanted his company and said, "Stay with us, because it will soon be dark."

He accepted and followed them all the way home. There they prepared something to eat and sat at the table together. Then Jesus took bread, recited the prayer of blessing, broke it, and gave it to them. At that moment they recognized him, but he had already vanished from their sight.

They had no doubts. It was Jesus! He was alive! They forgot their weariness and hurried back to Jerusalem to announce it to the others. They went to the place where the apostles and other disciples had gathered and found them all very excited. "The Lord has truly risen! He appeared to Simon!" they were saying as soon as they saw the two from Emmaus enter. Then Cleopas and his companion told them of having met Jesus along the way and of having recognized him when he broke the bread.

DOUBTING THOMAS

While they were still gathered in that house, with the doors barred for fear of the guards, Jesus appeared among them, saying, "Peace be with you." The disciples looked at him in shock.

Jesus said, "Do not be afraid. It's me, in the flesh. I'm not a ghost. Touch me." Now they smiled happily, but they still did not dare believe it was him.

Then Jesus said, "Do you have something to eat?" They gave him some roasted fish and he ate it in front of them.

Thomas, one of the apostles, was not with them at that time. When his friends told him later what had happened, he replied, "Until I see the marks of the nails for myself and I can touch his wounds, I will not believe your words."

Eight days later they were in the house again, and this time Thomas was there, too.

Jesus came again to them, "Peace be with you." Then he turned to Thomas, saying, "Put your hand on my wounds and believe in me." Thomas replied, "My Lord and my God!"

Jesus said, "You believed because you saw me! Blessed are those who have believed in me without having seen me."

BACK TO THE LAKE SHORE

The apostles returned to Galilee, to the shores of Sea of Tiberias. They felt the need to retrace their history with Jesus, starting from the place where the friendship with him had begun.
One evening Peter said to the others, "I'm going fishing."
They went out with him in the boat, but that night they did not catch anything.
In the first light of dawn, they saw a man on the shore who asked them, "Do you have anything to eat?" They answered no.
The man said, "Cast the net on the right side of the boat." They did as he had said and the net was filled with fish. Then John recognized him and said, "It is the Lord." Peter threw himself into the water, swimming to the shore, and the others followed him with

the boat full of fish. On the beach, Jesus had lit a fire. There was some fish roasting and some bread ready. Jesus said, "Bring some of the fish you have just caught and come and eat something."

They sat around the fire in silence and Jesus fed them. They looked at him full of joy, and no one dared ask him, "Is it really you?" Their hearts knew with certainty that it was the Lord.

After they had eaten, Jesus turned to Peter and said, "Peter, do you love me more than all of them?" Peter answered him, "Yes, Lord, you know that I love you." Jesus once again asked, "Peter, do you love me?" And Peter answered, "Yes, Lord, you know that I love you." Then for the third time Jesus asked, "Peter, do you love me?" Then Peter remembered how he had pretended not to know Jesus three times, and he said, "Lord, you know everything. You know that, despite what I am and what I've done, I love you."

Jesus said, "Take care of my sheep. I entrust them to you."

THE ASCENSION OF JESUS

After his resurrection, Jesus appeared many times to his disciples. After forty days, they went to a mountain in Galilee that Jesus had indicated to them.

When they saw him, they bowed, and Jesus spoke with them for the last time. "Now go and announce my kingdom to all the peoples of the earth. Baptize them in the name of the Father, of the Son, and of the Holy Spirit, and teach them all that I have told you. I will not leave you alone. I will be with you every day, until the end of the world."

As he was saying these words, Jesus was lifted off the ground and ascended into the sky, until a cloud hid him from their sight.

PENTECOST

After Jesus ascended into heaven, the apostles returned to
Jerusalem. With Mary and the other disciples, they gathered to pray
in the room where they had dinner with him for the last time, and
that place had become their common house. The Lord had told them
to await his greatest gift: the Holy Spirit.
At the suggestion of Peter, they decided to elect a new apostle
to take the place of Judas, so that the group of those who first
followed Jesus was again twelve. Two were proposed: Joseph,
nicknamed Justus, and Matthias. Then they prayed, "Lord, you
who know the heart of all, show us which one you have chosen."
They cast lots and the lot fell to Matthias, who from that
moment was considered one of the apostles.
Fifty days after Easter they were together. It was the day of
Pentecost, the feast when the Jews remembered the gift of
the covenant with the Lord and the delivery of the tablets of
the law. Suddenly, a strong wind rose with a roar like thunder.
A fire lit up the room and from the fire many little flames came and

rested on each one of them. It was the Holy Spirit promised by Jesus.

Then they went out into the city without fear and announced the great works of God of which they had been witnesses. But the wonders were not finished yet.

Attracted by all that noise, a large crowd had gathered around the house. Many were foreigners who had come to Jerusalem from every corner of the Mediterranean for the feast of Pentecost. They spoke different languages and dialects, yet each of them heard the apostles speaking in their own language. "How is it possible?" they said to each other in amazement. Others said, "Maybe they're drunk!"

The apostles also understood the languages of foreigners, and Peter stood up to speak. He said, "We are not drunk! We are talking about Jesus, the Savior announced by the prophets, who was crucified and rose from the dead. In him the Lord has fulfilled the promise made to our fathers. Convert and be baptized, and you will also receive the gift of the Holy Spirit." That day many believed and were baptized.

STEPHEN, THE FIRST MARTYR

The disciples of Jesus lived together with joy and simplicity of heart.
They listened to the teaching of the apostles, prayed, and broke
the bread in memory of Jesus. None of them were poor, because
they all shared what they could, and the fruit of their charity was
distributed by the apostles according to the need of each person.
When the number of believers increased, some among them
felt neglected. So the apostles convened an assembly and said,
"Brothers, we cannot take care of everything ourselves. Select
from among yourselves some men of faith who are well respected
by all, to whom to entrust daily tasks and assistance to the needy.
And we will continue to proclaim the word of God." Everyone agreed,
and a group of seven men was chosen. They were called deacons,
meaning "those who serve." Stephen, one of the seven deacons,
immediately distinguished himself from others.

He worked miracles and wonders by the power of the Holy Spirit.
Many who listened to him teaching converted to the faith in the
Risen Jesus.
Out of hatred and envy, some made false accusations against
Stephen, saying, "He blasphemies and speaks against the law!"
And they dragged him before the court of priests.
"Is that true?" the high priest asked him.
Stephen replied, "You have received the law and you do not observe
it! You did not even recognize in Jesus the Savior, the Lord of life."
Then, looking at the sky, he said, "Behold, I see the heavens opened
and the Son of Man standing at the right hand of God." Then his
enemies, full of anger, hurled themselves upon him, shouting at him.
They grabbed him, took him out of the city, and began to stone him.
A young man called Saul guarded the cloaks of the executioners.
Stephen meanwhile prayed, "Lord Jesus, receive my spirit."
Then, falling to the ground, he cried out, "Lord, forgive them this
sin." And he died, witnessing with his life his faith in Jesus.

GOD HAS NO FAVORITES

After Stephen's death, the Christians of Jerusalem were persecuted. Even Saul hunted them, going to their homes to arrest them. Many were forced to leave the city, but wherever they went they continued to announce the good news of Jesus. Among these was Philip, a deacon who performed miracles and healings in the name of Jesus in the cities of Samaria, which were despised by the Jews. One day, while he was on the road, he came across a chariot and he heard a man read a passage from the prophet Isaiah: "Like a lamb led to the slaughter, or a sheep silent before shearers, he did not open his mouth." He was an Ethiopian, minister of the queen of Ethiopia and administrator of all her treasures.

"Do you understand what you are reading?" Philip asked him. "How can I understand if nobody teaches me?" replied the Ethiopian. Philip, guided by the Holy Spirit, got into the chariot and told him about Jesus. The Ethiopian listened attentively and, when the

chariot passed near a stream, he stopped and said to Philip, "Let's stop, and you can baptize me!" They both went down into the water and Philip baptized him. Then the Ethiopian, full of joy, continued on his way, bringing the good news about Jesus to Ethiopia.

The community of believers was increasingly enriched with new people and experiences.

At that time in Caesarea, near the sea, lived a Roman centurion named Cornelius. He was a good man who gave many alms and prayed to God. One day an angel appeared to him saying, "Cornelius! God has listened to your prayers. Send your servants to call a man named Peter and listen to what he will tell you."

After a few days the servants returned accompanied by Peter. Cornelius was waiting for him with all his family and his closest friends. As soon as he saw him, he went to meet him and said, "We are here to listen to what the Lord has to say."

"Now I understand that God does not have preferences, but welcomes those who love him and practice justice, whatever nation they belong to," Peter said, and he told about how Jesus died and rose again for the salvation of all people. As he spoke, the Holy Spirit descended upon those who were listening to him. "If you have received the Spirit, who can prevent you from also being baptized in the name of Jesus?" And so he baptized them all.

THE CONVERSION OF SAUL

Saul persecuted the disciples of Jesus with great determination. He even asked the high priest for permission to go to Damascus to arrest the Christians of that city, to take them prisoners and bring them back to Jerusalem.

While he was on his way to Damascus, he was suddenly dazzled by a great light. He fell to the ground and heard a voice saying, "Saul, Saul, why are you persecuting me?"

He replied, "Who are you, sir?"

And the voice said, "I am Jesus whom you are persecuting."

Saul's companions were amazed, and they looked around without understanding where the voice came from. Saul got up, but realized he had gone blind. He had himself led to Damascus where he remained for three days praying, without eating or drinking. In Damascus lived Ananias, a disciple of Jesus. The Lord appeared to him and said, "Go and look for a man named Saul. He has become blind. I want you to heal him."

Ananias replied, "Lord, I know that man. He harmed our brothers in Jerusalem very badly and now he's here after us too."

But the Lord said, "Do as I tell you. I chose him to make my name known to all the peoples of the earth."

Ananias obeyed. He presented himself before Saul, laid his hands on him and said, "Brother Saul, Jesus has sent me to you so that you may regain your sight and be filled with the Holy Spirit." Immediately something like scales fell from Saul's eyes and his sight was restored. He was baptized and from that moment he never left Jesus again.

PAUL'S TRAVELS

Since Jesus had told Saul that he was one with the Christians whom he had been persecuting, Saul wanted nothing more than to make Jesus' name known everywhere. He walked the roads of the Roman empire, traveled by sea, with different companions, going from city to city to announce that Jesus was the Savior. He also took the name Paul, a common name in the Greek and Roman world, to make connections with everyone he met easier. New Christian communities were born from his preaching and to these new believers, whom he considered to be sons and daughters, Paul wrote some beautiful letters to make them feel his closeness and to support them in their faith.

Among the communities that were dear to him was Corinth, the great Greek city famous for its port, but also for its corruption. In Corinth were merchants, artisans, slaves, sailors, and adventurers from every corner of the world. When Paul arrived here for the first time, he went to the shop of Aquila and Priscilla, two spouses who made curtains, to ask for work so he could support himself. It was the beginning of a friendship that lasted a lifetime.

"Do not be afraid," the Lord had told him. "I am with you. Many in this city are waiting for me." In a short time that small group of friends became a large community.

To the beloved Christians of Corinth, Paul wrote, "Brothers and sisters, be joyful, correct one another, and be courageous with each other in difficulties. Get along and be at peace with each other, and the God of love and peace will be with you."

THE HEAVENLY JERUSALEM

It had been many years since the day the apostles, after
receiving the gift of the Holy Spirit, had begun to announce to
all men and women the word of Jesus. Peter and Paul had died
in Rome, executed during the persecutions. The other apostles,
scattered throughout the world, had also died bearing witness
to their faith.

Only one survived, John, who was now very old and exiled on
the island of Patmos, in the Aegean Sea.

To give comfort to those who still suffered because of violence
and injustice, John wrote a book called Revelation, a mysterious
book, which contained symbols, dreams, and visions concerning
the history of the world.

In John's vision, a great battle took place in the sky between
the forces of good and evil. The battle ended with the triumph
of the Lamb, a symbol of Jesus who sacrificed himself for the
love of all people and who rose again, defeating death once and
for all. Now the world appeared to be made new. From heaven
came down the holy city of Jerusalem, shining with light like
a jewel, with the throne of the Lamb at the center. A river of
living water, crystal clear, flowed from the throne and nourished
the lands it passed through.

A powerful voice said, "This is the home of God among people!
God will live among them. He will wipe away all the tears from
their eyes and there will be no more death, mourning, or cries
of pain because everything has been made new."

CONTENTS

NEW TESTAMENT